GLENCOE
MATHEMATICS

Algebra 1

Chapter 5
Resource Masters

Mc Graw Hill **Glencoe
McGraw-Hill**

New York, New York
Columbus, Ohio
Chicago, Illinois
Peoria, Illinois
Woodland Hills, California

CONSUMABLE WORKBOOKS Many of the worksheets contained in the Chapter Resource Masters booklets are available as consumable workbooks in both English and Spanish.

Study Guide and Intervention Workbook	0-07-827753-1
Study Guide and Intervention Workbook (Spanish)	0-07-827754-X
Skills Practice Workbook	0-07-827747-7
Skills Practice Workbook (Spanish)	0-07-827749-3
Practice Workbook	0-07-827748-5
Practice Workbook (Spanish)	0-07-827750-7

ANSWERS FOR WORKBOOKS The answers for Chapter 5 of these workbooks can be found in the back of this Chapter Resource Masters booklet.

StudentWorks™ This CD-ROM includes the entire Student Edition text along with the English workbooks listed above.

TeacherWorks™ All of the materials found in this booklet are included for viewing and printing in the *Glencoe Algebra 1 TeacherWorks* CD-ROM.

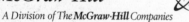

Glencoe/McGraw-Hill

A Division of The McGraw-Hill Companies

Send all inquiries to:
The McGraw-Hill Companies
8787 Orion Place
Columbus, OH 43240-4027

ISBN: 0-07-827729-9

Glencoe Algebra 1
Chapter 5 Resource Masters

6 7 8 9 10 024 11 10 09 08 07 06

Contents

Teacher's Guide to Using the Chapter 5 Resource Masters

The *Fast File* Chapter Resource system allows you to conveniently file the resources you use most often. The *Chapter 5 Resource Masters* includes the core materials needed for Chapter 5. These materials include worksheets, extensions, and assessment options. The answers for these pages appear at the back of this booklet.

All of the materials found in this booklet are included for viewing and printing in the *Algebra 1 TeacherWorks* CD-ROM.

Vocabulary Builder
Pages vii–viii include a student study tool that presents up to twenty of the key vocabulary terms from the chapter. Students are to record definitions and/or examples for each term. You may suggest that students highlight or star the terms with which they are not familiar.

WHEN TO USE Give these pages to students before beginning Lesson 5-1. Encourage them to add these pages to their Algebra Study Notebook. Remind them to add definitions and examples as they complete each lesson.

Study Guide and Intervention
Each lesson in *Algebra 1* addresses two objectives. There is one Study Guide and Intervention master for each objective.

WHEN TO USE Use these masters as reteaching activities for students who need additional reinforcement. These pages can also be used in conjunction with the Student Edition as an instructional tool for students who have been absent.

Skills Practice
There is one master for each lesson. These provide computational practice at a basic level.

WHEN TO USE These masters can be used with students who have weaker mathematics backgrounds or need additional reinforcement.

Practice
There is one master for each lesson. These problems more closely follow the structure of the Practice and Apply section of the Student Edition exercises. These exercises are of average difficulty.

WHEN TO USE These provide additional practice options or may be used as homework for second day teaching of the lesson.

Reading to Learn Mathematics
One master is included for each lesson. The first section of each master asks questions about the opening paragraph of the lesson in the Student Edition. Additional questions ask students to interpret the context of and relationships among terms in the lesson. Finally, students are asked to summarize what they have learned using various representation techniques.

WHEN TO USE This master can be used as a study tool when presenting the lesson or as an informal reading assessment after presenting the lesson. It is also a helpful tool for ELL (English Language Learner) students.

Enrichment
There is one extension master for each lesson. These activities may extend the concepts in the lesson, offer an historical or multicultural look at the concepts, or widen students' perspectives on the mathematics they are learning. These are not written exclusively for honors students, but are accessible for use with all levels of students.

WHEN TO USE These may be used as extra credit, short-term projects, or as activities for days when class periods are shortened.

Assessment Options

The assessment masters in the *Chapter 5 Resources Masters* offer a wide range of assessment tools for intermediate and final assessment. The following lists describe each assessment master and its intended use.

Chapter Assessment

CHAPTER TESTS

- *Form 1* contains multiple-choice questions and is intended for use with basic level students.

- *Forms 2A and 2B* contain multiple-choice questions aimed at the average level student. These tests are similar in format to offer comparable testing situations.

- *Forms 2C and 2D* are composed of free-response questions aimed at the average level student. These tests are similar in format to offer comparable testing situations. Grids with axes are provided for questions assessing graphing skills.

- *Form 3* is an advanced level test with free-response questions. Grids without axes are provided for questions assessing graphing skills.

  All of the above tests include a free-response Bonus question.

- The **Open-Ended Assessment** includes performance assessment tasks that are suitable for all students. A scoring rubric is included for evaluation guidelines. Sample answers are provided for assessment.

- A **Vocabulary Test**, suitable for all students, includes a list of the vocabulary words in the chapter and ten questions assessing students' knowledge of those terms. This can also be used in conjunction with one of the chapter tests or as a review worksheet.

Intermediate Assessment

- Four free-response **quizzes** are included to offer assessment at appropriate intervals in the chapter.

- A **Mid-Chapter Test** provides an option to assess the first half of the chapter. It is composed of both multiple-choice and free-response questions.

Continuing Assessment

- The **Cumulative Review** provides students an opportunity to reinforce and retain skills as they proceed through their study of Algebra 1. It can also be used as a test. This master includes free-response questions.

- The **Standardized Test Practice** offers continuing review of algebra concepts in various formats, which may appear on the standardized tests that they may encounter. This practice includes multiple-choice, grid-in, and quantitative-comparison questions. Bubble-in and grid-in answer sections are provided on the master.

Answers

- Page A1 is an answer sheet for the Standardized Test Practice questions that appear in the Student Edition on pages 314–315. This improves students' familiarity with the answer formats they may encounter in test taking.

- The answers for the lesson-by-lesson masters are provided as reduced pages with answers appearing in red.

- Full-size answer keys are provided for the assessment masters in this booklet.

5 Reading to Learn Mathematics
Vocabulary Builder

This is an alphabetical list of the key vocabulary terms you will learn in Chapter 5. As you study the chapter, complete each term's definition or description. Remember to add the page number where you found the term. Add these pages to your Algebra Study Notebook to review vocabulary at the end of the chapter.

Vocabulary Term	Found on Page	Definition/Description/Example
constant of variation		
direct variation		
family of graphs		
line of fit		
linear extrapolation ihk·STRA·puh·LAY·shun		
linear interpolation ihn·TUHR·puh·LAY·shun		
negative correlation KAWR·uh·LAY·shun		
parallel lines		

(continued on the next page)

5 **Reading to Learn Mathematics**

Vocabulary Builder (continued)

Vocabulary Term	Found on Page	Definition/Description/Example
perpendicular lines PUHR·puhn·DIH·kyuh·luhr		
point-slope form		
positive correlation		
rate of change		
scatter plot		
slope		
slope-intercept form IHN·tuhr·SEHPT		

Glencoe Algebra 1

5-1 Study Guide and Intervention
Slope

Find Slope

Slope of a Line	$m = \dfrac{\text{rise}}{\text{run}}$ or $m = \dfrac{y_2 - y_1}{x_2 - x_1}$, where (x_1, y_1) and (x_2, y_2) are the coordinates of any two points on a nonvertical line

Example 1 **Find the slope of the line that passes through $(-3, 5)$ and $(4, -2)$.**

Let $(-3, 5) = (x_1, y_1)$ and $(4, -2) = (x_2, y_2)$.

$m = \dfrac{y_2 - y_1}{x_2 - x_1}$ Slope formula

$= \dfrac{-2 - 5}{4 - (-3)}$ $y_2 = -2, y_1 = 5, x_2 = 4, x_1 = -3$

$= \dfrac{-7}{7}$ Simplify.

$= -1$

Example 2 **Find the value of r so that the line through $(10, r)$ and $(3, 4)$ has a slope of $-\dfrac{2}{7}$.**

$m = \dfrac{y_2 - y_1}{x_2 - x_1}$ Slope formula

$-\dfrac{2}{7} = \dfrac{4 - r}{3 - 10}$ $m = -\dfrac{2}{7}, y_2 = 4, y_1 = r, x_2 = 3, x_1 = 10$

$-\dfrac{2}{7} = \dfrac{4 - r}{-7}$ Simplify.

$-2(-7) = 7(4 - r)$ Cross multiply.

$14 = 28 - 7r$ Distributive Property

$-14 = -7r$ Subtract 28 from each side.

$2 = r$ Divide each side by -7.

Exercises

Find the slope of the line that passes through each pair of points.

1. $(4, 9), (1, 6)$

2. $(-4, -1), (-2, -5)$

3. $(-4, -1), (-4, -5)$

4. $(2, 1), (8, 9)$

5. $(14, -8), (7, -6)$

6. $(4, -3), (8, -3)$

7. $(1, -2), (6, 2)$

8. $(2, 5), (6, 2)$

9. $(4, 3.5), (-4, 3.5)$

Determine the value of r so the line that passes through each pair of points has the given slope.

10. $(6, 8), (r, -2), m = 1$

11. $(-1, -3), (7, r), m = \dfrac{3}{4}$

12. $(2, 8), (r, -4)\ m = -3$

13. $(7, -5), (6, r), m = 0$

14. $(r, 4), (7, 1), m = \dfrac{3}{4}$

15. $(7, 5), (r, 9), m = 6$

16. $(10, r), (3, 4), m = -\dfrac{2}{7}$

17. $(10, 4), (-2, r), m = -0.5$

18. $(r, 3), (7, r), m = -\dfrac{1}{5}$

5-1 **Study Guide and Intervention** (continued)

Slope

Rate of Change The **rate of change** tells, on average, how a quantity is changing over time. Slope describes a rate of change.

Example **POPULATION** The graph shows the population growth in China.

a. **Find the rates of change for 1950–1975 and for 1975–2000.**

1950–1975: $\dfrac{\text{change in population}}{\text{change in time}} = \dfrac{0.93 - 0.55}{1975 - 1950}$

$= \dfrac{0.38}{25}$ or 0.0152

1975–2000: $\dfrac{\text{change in population}}{\text{change in time}} = \dfrac{1.24 - 0.93}{2000 - 1975}$

$= \dfrac{0.31}{25}$ or 0.0124

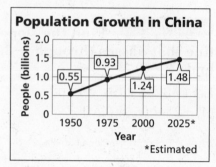

Population Growth in China

Source: United Nations Population Division

b. **Explain the meaning of the slope in each case.**

From 1950–1975, the growth was 0.0152 billion per year, or 15.2 million per year.
From 1975–2000, the growth was 0.0124 billion per year, or 12.4 million per year.

c. **How are the different rates of change shown on the graph?**

There is a greater vertical change for 1950–1975 than for 1975–2000. Therefore, the section of the graph for 1950–1975 has a steeper slope.

Exercises

LONGEVITY The graph shows the predicted life expectancy for men and women born in a given year.

1. Find the rates of change for women from 2000–2025 and 2025–2050.

2. Find the rates of change for men from 2000–2025 and 2025–2050.

3. Explain the meaning of your results in Exercises 1 and 2.

4. What pattern do you see in the increase with each 25-year period?

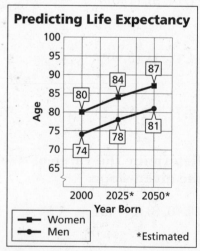

Predicting Life Expectancy

Source: *USA TODAY*

5. Make a prediction for the life expectancy for 2050–2075. Explain how you arrived at your prediction.

5-1 Skills Practice

Slope

Find the slope of the line that passes through each pair of points.

1.
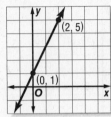

2.
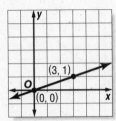

3.
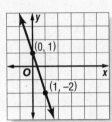

4. $(2, 5), (3, 6)$

5. $(6, 1), (-6, 1)$

6. $(4, 6), (4, 8)$

7. $(5, 2), (5, -2)$

8. $(2, 5), (-3, -5)$

9. $(9, 8), (7, -8)$

10. $(-5, -8), (-8, 1)$

11. $(-3, 10), (-3, 7)$

12. $(17, 18), (18, 17)$

13. $(-6, -4), (4, 1)$

14. $(10, 0), (-2, 4)$

15. $(2, -1), (-8, -2)$

16. $(5, -9), (3, -2)$

17. $(12, 6), (3, -5)$

18. $(-4, 5), (-8, -5)$

19. $(-5, 6), (7, -8)$

Find the value of r so the line that passes through each pair of points has the given slope.

20. $(r, 3), (5, 9), m = 2$

21. $(5, 9), (r, -3), m = -4$

22. $(r, 2), (6, 3), m = \frac{1}{2}$

23. $(r, 4), (7, 1), m = \frac{3}{4}$

24. $(5, 3), (r, -5), m = 4$

25. $(7, r), (4, 6), m = 0$

Lesson 5-1

5-1 Practice

Slope

Find the slope of the line that passes through each pair of points.

1.
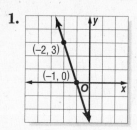

2.
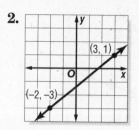

3.
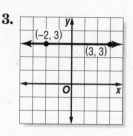

4. $(6, 3), (7, -4)$

5. $(-9, -3), (-7, -5)$

6. $(6, -2), (5, -4)$

7. $(7, -4), (4, 8)$

8. $(-7, 8), (-7, 5)$

9. $(5, 9), (3, 9)$

10. $(15, 2), (-6, 5)$

11. $(3, 9), (-2, 8)$

12. $(-2, -5), (7, 8)$

13. $(12, 10), (12, 5)$

14. $(0.2, -0.9), (0.5, -0.9)$

15. $\left(\frac{7}{3}, \frac{4}{3}\right), \left(-\frac{1}{3}, \frac{2}{3}\right)$

Find the value of r so the line that passes through each pair of points has the given slope.

16. $(-2, r), (6, 7), m = \frac{1}{2}$

17. $(-4, 3), (r, 5), m = \frac{1}{4}$

18. $(-3, -4), (-5, r), m = -\frac{9}{2}$

19. $(-5, r), (1, 3), m = \frac{7}{6}$

20. $(1, 4), (r, 5), m$ undefined

21. $(-7, 2), (-8, r), m = -5$

22. $(r, 7), (11, 8), m = -\frac{1}{5}$

23. $(r, 2), (5, r), m = 0$

24. **ROOFING** The *pitch* of a roof is the number of feet the roof rises for each 12 feet horizontally. If a roof has a pitch of 8, what is its slope expressed as a positive number?

25. **SALES** A daily newspaper had 12,125 subscribers when it began publication. Five years later it had 10,100 subscribers. What is the average yearly rate of change in the number of subscribers for the five-year period?

Reading to Learn Mathematics

Slope

Pre-Activity **Why is slope important in architecture?**

Read the introduction to Lesson 5-1 at the top of page 256 in your textbook. Then complete the definition of slope and fill in the boxes on the graph with the words *rise* and *run*.

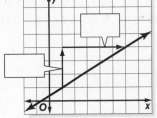

slope = —————

In this graph, the rise is _____ units, and the run is _____ units.

Thus, the slope of this line is $\dfrac{\text{units}}{\text{units}}$ or —.

Reading the Lesson

1. Describe each type of slope and include a sketch.

Type of Slope	Description of Graph	Sketch
positive		
negative		
zero		
undefined		

2. Describe how each expression is related to *slope*.

a. $\dfrac{y_2 - y_1}{x_2 - x_1}$

b. $\dfrac{\text{rise}}{\text{run}}$

c. $\dfrac{\$52,000 \text{ increase in spending}}{26 \text{ months}}$

Helping You Remember

3. The word *rise* is usually associated with going up. Sometimes going from one point on the graph does not involve a rise and a run but a fall and a run. Describe how you could select points so that it is always a rise from the first point to the second point.

Lesson 5-1

5-1 **Enrichment**

Treasure Hunt with Slopes

Using the definition of slope, draw lines with the slopes listed
below. A correct solution will trace the route to the treasure.

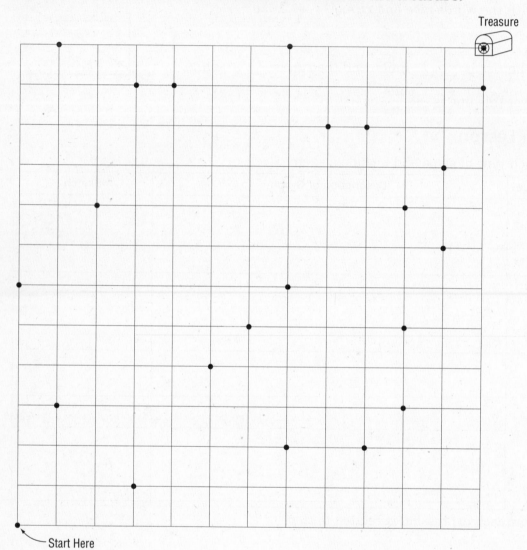

Treasure

Start Here

1. 3	**2.** $\frac{1}{4}$	**3.** $-\frac{2}{5}$	**4.** 0
5. 1	**6.** -1	**7.** no slope	**8.** $\frac{2}{7}$
9. $\frac{3}{2}$	**10.** $\frac{1}{3}$	**11.** $-\frac{3}{4}$	**12.** 3

Glencoe Algebra 1

5-2 Study Guide and Intervention

Slope and Direct Variation

Direct Variation A **direct variation** is described by an equation of the form $y = kx$, where $k \neq 0$. We say that *y varies directly as x*. In the equation $y = kx$, k is the **constant of variation**.

Lesson 5-2

Example 1 Name the constant of variation for the equation. Then find the slope of the line that passes through the pair of points.

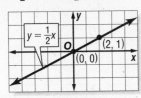

For $y = \frac{1}{2}x$, the constant of variation is $\frac{1}{2}$.

$$m = \frac{y_2 - y_1}{x_2 - x_1} \quad \text{Slope formula}$$

$$= \frac{1 - 0}{2 - 0} \quad (x_1, y_1) = (0, 0), (x_2, y_2) = (2, 1)$$

$$= \frac{1}{2} \quad \text{Simplify.}$$

The slope is $\frac{1}{2}$.

Example 2 Suppose *y* varies directly as *x*, and *y* = 30 when *x* = 5.

a. Write a direct variation equation that relates *x* and *y*.

Find the value of k.

$y = kx$ Direct variation equation

$30 = k(5)$ Replace *y* with 30 and *x* with 5.

$6 = k$ Divide each side by 5.

Therefore, the equation is $y = 6x$.

b. Use the direct variation equation to find *x* when *y* = 18.

$y = 6x$ Direct variation equation

$18 = 6x$ Replace *y* with 18.

$3 = x$ Divide each side by 6.

Therefore, $x = 3$ when $y = 18$.

Exercises

Name the constant of variation for each equation. Then determine the slope of the line that passes through each pair of points.

1.
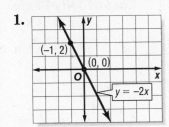

2.
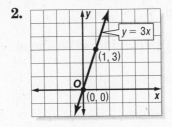

3.
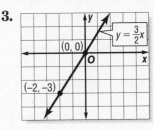

Write a direct variation equation that relates *x* to *y*. Assume that *y* varies directly as *x*. Then solve.

4. If $y = 4$ when $x = 2$, find y when $x = 16$.

5. If $y = 9$ when $x = -3$, find x when $y = 6$.

6. If $y = -4.8$ when $x = -1.6$, find x when $y = -24$.

7. If $y = \frac{1}{4}$ when $x = \frac{1}{8}$, find x when $y = \frac{3}{16}$.

5-2 Study Guide and Intervention (continued)

Slope and Direct Variation

Solve Problems The **distance formula** $d = rt$ is a direct variation equation. In the formula, distance d varies directly as time t, and the rate r is the constant of variation.

Example TRAVEL A family drove their car 225 miles in 5 hours.

a. Write a direct variation equation to find the distance traveled for any number of hours.

Use given values for d and t to find r.

$d = rt$ Original equation
$225 = r(5)$ $d = 225$ and $t = 5$
$45 = r$ Divide each side by 5.

Therefore, the direct variation equation is $d = 45t$.

b. Graph the equation.

The graph of $d = 45t$ passes through the origin with slope 45.

$$m = \frac{45}{1} \quad \frac{\text{rise}}{\text{run}}$$

✓CHECK (5, 225) lies on the graph.

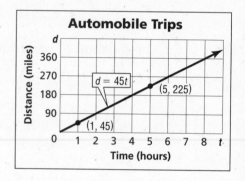

c. Estimate how many hours it would take the family to drive 360 miles.

$d = 45t$ Original equation
$360 = 45t$ Replace d with 360.
$t = 8$ Divide each side by 45.

Therefore, it will take 8 hours to drive 360 miles.

Exercises

RETAIL The total cost C of bulk jelly beans is $4.49 times the number of pounds p.

1. Write a direct variation equation that relates the variables.

2. Graph the equation on the grid at the right.

3. Find the cost of $\frac{3}{4}$ pound of jelly beans.

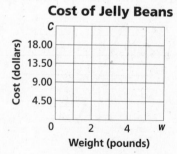

CHEMISTRY Charles's Law states that, at a constant pressure, volume of a gas V varies directly as its temperature T. A volume of 4 cubic feet of a certain gas has a temperature of 200° (absolute temperature).

4. Write a direct variation equation that relates the variables.

5. Graph the equation on the grid at the right.

6. Find the volume of the same gas at 250° (absolute temperature).

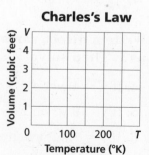

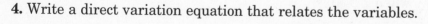

5-2 # Skills Practice

Slope and Direct Variation

Lesson 5-2

Name the constant of variation for each equation. Then determine the slope of the line that passes through each pair of points.

1.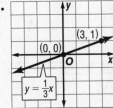

2.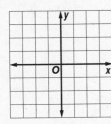

3.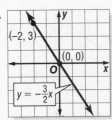

Graph each equation.

4. $y = 3x$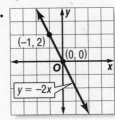

5. $y = -\dfrac{3}{4}x$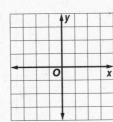

6. $y = \dfrac{2}{5}x$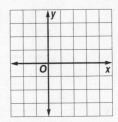

Write a direct variation equation that relates x and y. Assume that y varies directly as x. Then solve.

7. If $y = -8$ when $x = -2$, find x when $y = 32$.

8. If $y = 45$ when $x = 15$, find x when $y = 15$.

9. If $y = -4$ when $x = 2$, find y when $x = -6$.

10. If $y = -9$ when $x = 3$, find y when $x = -5$.

11. If $y = 4$ when $x = 16$, find y when $x = 6$.

12. If $y = 12$ when $x = 18$, find x when $y = -16$.

Write a direct variation equation that relates the variables. Then graph the equation.

13. **TRAVEL** The total cost C of gasoline is \$1.80 times the number of gallons g.

Gasoline Cost

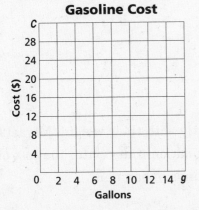

14. **SHIPPING** The number of delivered toys T is 3 times the total number of crates c.

Toys Shipped

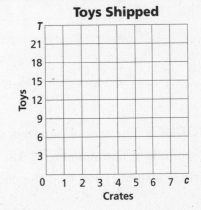

NAME _____ DATE _____ PERIOD _____

5-2 Practice

Slope and Direct Variation

Name the constant of variation for each equation. Then determine the slope of the line that passes through each pair of points.

1.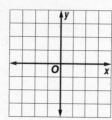

2.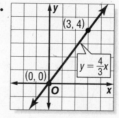

3.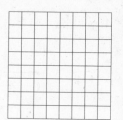

Graph each equation.

4. $y = -2x$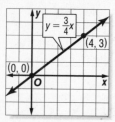

5. $y = \dfrac{6}{5}x$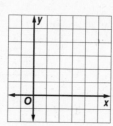

6. $y = -\dfrac{5}{3}x$

Write a direct variation equation that relates x and y. Assume that y varies directly as x. Then solve.

7. If $y = 7.5$ when $x = 0.5$, find y when $x = -0.3$.

8. If $y = 80$ when $x = 32$, find x when $y = 100$.

9. If $y = \dfrac{3}{4}$ when $x = 24$, find y when $x = 12$.

Write a direct variation equation that relates the variables. Then graph the equation.

10. **MEASURE** The width W of a rectangle is two thirds of the length ℓ.

11. **TICKETS** The total cost C of tickets is $4.50 times the number of tickets t.

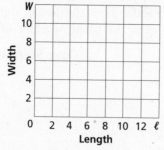

Rectangle Dimensions

12. **PRODUCE** The cost of bananas varies directly with their weight. Miguel bought $3\dfrac{1}{2}$ pounds of bananas for $1.12. Write an equation that relates the cost of the bananas to their weight. Then find the cost of $4\dfrac{1}{4}$ pounds of bananas.

© Glencoe/McGraw-Hill   **290**   Glencoe Algebra 1

5-2 Reading to Learn Mathematics

Slope and Direct Variation

Pre-Activity   **How is slope related to your shower?**

Read the introduction to Lesson 5-2 at the top of page 264 in your textbook.

- How do the numbers in the table relate to the graph shown?

- Think about the first sentence. What does it mean to say that a standard showerhead uses about 6 gallons of water per minute?

Reading the Lesson

1. What is the form of a direct variation equation?

2. How is the constant of variation related to slope?

3. The expression "y varies directly as x" can be written as the equation $y = kx$. How would you write an equation for "w varies directly as the square of t"?

4. For each situation, write an equation with the proper constant of variation.

   a. The distance d varies directly as time t, and a cheetah can travel 88 feet in 1 second.

   b. The perimeter p of a pentagon with all sides of equal length varies directly as the length s of a side of the pentagon. A pentagon has 5 sides.

   c. The wages W earned by an employee vary directly with the number of hours h that are worked. Enrique earned $172.50 for 23 hours of work.

Helping You Remember

5. Look up the word *constant* in a dictionary. How does this definition relate to the term constant of variation?

Lesson 5-2

5-2 Enrichment

nth Power Variation

An equation of the form $y = kx^n$, where $k \neq 0$, describes an nth power variation. The variable n can be replaced by 2 to indicate the second power of x (the square of x) or by 3 to indicate the third power of x (the cube of x).

Assume that the weight of a person of average build varies directly as the cube of that person's height. The equation of variation has the form $w = kh^3$.

The weight that a person's legs will support is proportional to the cross-sectional area of the leg bones. This area varies directly as the square of the person's height. The equation of variation has the form $s = kh^2$.

Answer each question.

1. For a person 6 feet tall who weighs 200 pounds, find a value for k in the equation $w = kh^3$.

2. Use your answer from Exercise 1 to predict the weight of a person who is 5 feet tall.

3. Find the value for k in the equation $w = kh^3$ for a baby who is 20 inches long and weighs 6 pounds.

4. How does your answer to Exercise 3 demonstrate that a baby is significantly fatter in proportion to its height than an adult?

5. For a person 6 feet tall who weighs 200 pounds, find a value for k in the equation $s = kh^2$.

6. For a baby who is 20 inches long and weighs 6 pounds, find an "infant value" for k in the equation $s = kh^2$.

7. According to the adult equation you found (Exercise 1), how much would an imaginary giant 20 feet tall weigh?

8. According to the adult equation for weight supported (Exercise 5), how much weight could a 20-foot tall giant's legs actually support?

9. What can you conclude from Exercises 7 and 8?

5-3 **Study Guide and Intervention**

Slope-Intercept Form

Slope-Intercept Form

Slope-Intercept Form	$y = mx + b$, where m is the given slope and b is the y-intercept

Example 1 Write an equation of the line whose slope is -4 and whose y-intercept is 3.

$y = mx + b$ Slope-intercept form
$y = -4x + 3$ Replace m with -4 and b with 3.

Example 2 Graph $3x - 4y = 8$.

$3x - 4y = 8$ Original equation

$-4y = -3x + 8$ Subtract $3x$ from each side.

$\dfrac{-4y}{-4} = \dfrac{-3x + 8}{-4}$ Divide each side by -4.

$y = \dfrac{3}{4}x - 2$ Simplify.

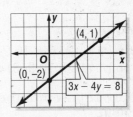

The y-intercept of $y = \dfrac{3}{4}x - 2$ is -2 and the slope is $\dfrac{3}{4}$. So graph the point $(0, -2)$. From this point, move up 3 units and right 4 units. Draw a line passing through both points.

Exercises

Write an equation of the line with the given slope and y-intercept.

1. slope: 8, y-intercept -3 **2.** slope: -2, y-intercept -1 **3.** slope: -1, y-intercept -7

Write an equation of the line shown in each graph.

4. 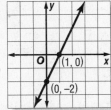   **5.** 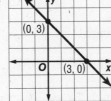   **6.**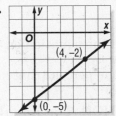

Graph each equation.

7. $y = 2x + 1$ **8.** $y = -3x + 2$ **9.** $y = -x - 1$

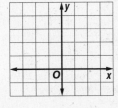   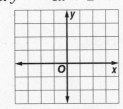   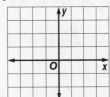

Lesson 5-3

5-3 Study Guide and Intervention (continued)

Slope-Intercept Form

Model Real-World Data

Example **MEDIA** Since 1997, the number of cable TV systems has decreased by an average rate of 121 systems per year. There were 10,943 systems in 1997.

a. Write a linear equation to find the average number of cable systems in any year after 1997.

The rate of change is -121 systems per year. In the first year, the number of systems was 10,943. Let N = the number of cable TV systems. Let x = the number of years after 1997. An equation is $N = -121x + 10,943$.

b. Graph the equation.

The graph of $N = -121x + 10,943$ is a line that passes through the point at (0, 10,943) and has a slope of -121.

c. Find the approximate number of cable TV systems in 2000.

$N = -121x + 10,943$	Original equation
$N = -121(3) + 10,943$	Replace x with 3.
$N = 10,580$	Simplify.

There were about 10,580 cable TV systems in 2000.

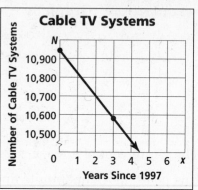

Cable TV Systems

Source: *The World Almanac*

Exercises

ENTERTAINMENT In 1995, 65.7% of all households with TV's in the U.S. subscribed to cable TV. Between 1995 and 1999, the percent increased by about 0.6% each year.

1. Write an equation to find the percent P of households that subscribed to cable TV for any year x between 1995 and 1999.

2. Graph the equation on the grid at the right.

3. Find the percent that subscribed to cable TV in 1999.

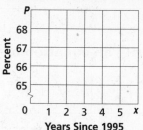

Percent of Households with TV Having Cable

Source: *The World Almanac*

POPULATION The population of the United States is projected to be 300 million by the year 2010. Between 2010 and 2050, the population is expected to increase by about 2.5 million per year.

4. Write an equation to find the population P in any year x between 2010 and 2050.

5. Graph the equation on the grid at the right.

6. Find the population in 2050.

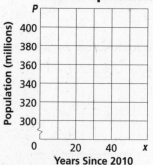

Projected United States Population

Source: *The World Almanac*

5-3 Skills Practice

Slope-Intercept Form

Write an equation of the line with the given slope and *y*-intercept.

1. slope: 5, *y*-intercept: −3

2. slope: −2, *y*-intercept: 7

3. slope: −6, *y*-intercept: −2

4. slope: 7, *y*-intercept: 1

5. slope: 3, *y*-intercept: 2

6. slope: −4, *y*-intercept: −9

7. slope: 1, *y*-intercept: −12

8. slope: 0, *y*-intercept: 8

Write an equation of the line shown in each graph.

9.
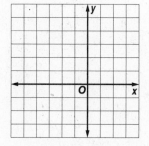

10.
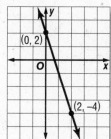

11.
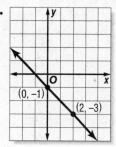

Graph each equation.

12. $y = x + 4$

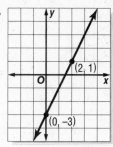

13. $y = -2x - 1$

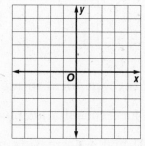

14. $x + y = -3$

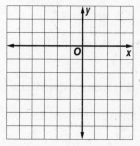

Write a linear equation in slope-intercept form to model each situation.

15. A video store charges $10 for a rental card plus $2 per rental.

16. A Norfolk pine is 18 inches tall and grows at a rate of 1.5 feet per year.

17. A Cairn terrier weighs 30 pounds and is on a special diet to lose 2 pounds per month.

18. An airplane at an altitude of 3000 feet descends at a rate of 500 feet per mile.

Lesson 5-3

5-3 Practice

Slope-Intercept Form

Write an equation of the line with the given slope and *y*-intercept.

1. slope: $\frac{1}{4}$, *y*-intercept: 3

2. slope: $\frac{3}{2}$, *y*-intercept: -4

3. slope: 1.5, *y*-intercept: -1

4. slope: -2.5, *y*-intercept: 3.5

Write an equation of the line shown in each graph.

5.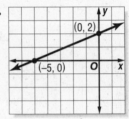

6.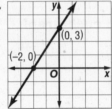

7.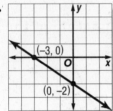

Graph each equation.

8. $y = -\frac{1}{2}x + 2$

9. $3y = 2x - 6$

10. $6x + 3y = 6$

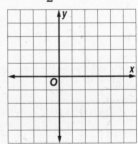

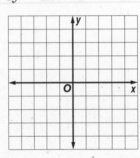

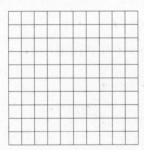

Write a linear equation in slope-intercept form to model each situation.

11. A computer technician charges $75 for a consultation plus $35 per hour.

12. The population of Pine Bluff is 6791 and is decreasing at the rate of 7 per year.

WRITING For Exercises 13–15, use the following information.

Carla has already written 10 pages of a novel. She plans to write 15 additional pages per month until she is finished.

13. Write an equation to find the total number of pages *P* written after any number of months *m*.

14. Graph the equation on the grid at the right.

15. Find the total number of pages written after 5 months.

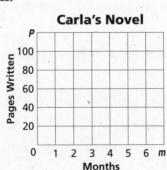

5-3 Reading to Learn Mathematics

Slope-Intercept Form

Pre-Activity **How is a *y*-intercept related to a flat fee?**

Read the introduction to Lesson 5-3 at the top of page 272 in your textbook.

- What point on the graph shows that the flat fee is $5.00?

- How does the rate of $0.10 per minute relate to the graph?

Reading the Lesson

1. Fill in the boxes with the correct words to describe what *m* and *b* represent.

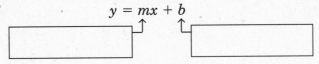

$$y = mx + b$$

2. What are the slope and *y*-intercept of a vertical line?

3. What are the slope and *y*-intercept of a horizontal line?

4. Read the problem. Then answer each part of the exercise.

A ruby-throated hummingbird weighs about 0.6 gram at birth and gains weight at a rate of about 0.2 gram per day until fully grown.

a. Write a verbal equation to show how the words are related to finding the average weight of a ruby-throated hummingbird at any given week. Use the words *weight at birth*, *rate of growth*, *weight*, and *weeks after birth*. Below the equation, fill in any values you know and put a question mark under the items that you do not know.

b. Define what variables to use for the unknown quantities.

c. Use the variables you defined and what you know from the problem to write an equation.

Helping You Remember

5. One way to remember something is to explain it to another person. Write how you would explain to someone the process for using the *y*-intercept and slope to graph a linear equation.

Lesson 5-3

5-3 Enrichment

Relating Slope-Intercept Form and Standard Forms

You have learned that slope can be defined in terms of $\dfrac{\text{rise}}{\text{run}}$ or $\dfrac{y_2 - y_1}{x_2 - x_1}$.

Another definition can be found from the standard from of a linear equation. Standard form is $Ax + By = C$, where A, B, and C are integers, $A \geq 0$, and A and B are not both zero.

1. Solve $Ax + By = C$ for y. Your answer should be written in slope-intercept form.

2. Use the slope-intercept equation you wrote in Exercise 1 to write expressions for the slope and the y-intercept in terms of A, B, and C.

Use the expressions in Exercise 2 above to find the slope and y-intercept of each equation.

3. $2x + y = -4$ 4. $4x + 3y = 24$

5. $4x + 6y = -36$ 6. $x - 3y = -27$

7. $x - 2y = 6$ 8. $4y = 20$

NAME _____ DATE _____ PERIOD _____

5-4 Study Guide and Intervention

Writing Equations in Slope-Intercept Form

Write an Equation Given the Slope and One Point

Example 1 Write an equation of a line that passes through $(-4, 2)$ with slope 3.

The line has slope 3. To find the y-intercept, replace m with 3 and (x, y) with $(-4, 2)$ in the slope-intercept form. Then solve for b.

$y = mx + b$ Slope-intercept form
$2 = 3(-4) + b$ $m = 3$, $y = 2$, and $x = -4$
$2 = -12 + b$ Multiply.
$14 = b$ Add 12 to each side.

Therefore, the equation is $y = 3x + 14$.

Example 2 Write an equation of the line that passes through $(-2, -1)$ with slope $\frac{1}{4}$.

The line has slope $\frac{1}{4}$. Replace m with $\frac{1}{4}$ and (x, y) with $(-2, -1)$ in the slope-intercept form.

$y = mx + b$ Slope-intercept form
$-1 = \frac{1}{4}(-2) + b$ $m = \frac{1}{4}$, $y = -1$, and $x = -2$
$-1 = -\frac{1}{2} + b$ Multiply.
$-\frac{1}{2} = b$ Add $\frac{1}{2}$ to each side.

Therefore, the equation is $y = \frac{1}{4}x - \frac{1}{2}$.

Exercises

Write an equation of the line that passes through each point with the given slope.

1.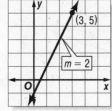

2.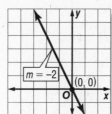

3.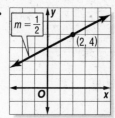

4. $(8, 2)$, $m = -\frac{3}{4}$

5. $(-1, -3)$, $m = 5$

6. $(4, -5)$, $m = -\frac{1}{2}$

7. $(-5, 4)$, $m = 0$

8. $(2, 2)$, $m = \frac{1}{2}$

9. $(1, -4)$, $m = -6$

10. Write an equation of a line that passes through the y-intercept -3 with slope 2.

11. Write an equation of a line that passes through the x-intercept 4 with slope -3.

12. Write an equation of a line that passes through the point $(0, 350)$ with slope $\frac{1}{5}$.

© Glencoe/McGraw-Hill   299   Glencoe Algebra 1

5-4 Study Guide and Intervention *(continued)*

Writing Equations in Slope-Intercept Form

Write an Equation Given Two Points

> **Example** Write an equation of the line that passes through (1, 2) and (3, −2).

Find the slope m. To find the y-intercept, replace m with its computed value and (x, y) with (1, 2) in the slope-intercept form. Then solve for b.

$m = \dfrac{y_2 - y_1}{x_2 - x_1}$ Slope formula

$m = \dfrac{-2 - 2}{3 - 1}$ $y_2 = -2, y_1 = 2, x_2 = 3, x_1 = 1$

$m = -2$ Simplify.

$y = mx + b$ Slope-intercept form

$2 = -2(1) + b$ Replace m with −2, y with 2, and x with 1.

$2 = -2 + b$ Multiply.

$4 = b$ Add 2 to each side.

Therefore, the equation is $y = -2x + 4$.

> **Exercises**

Write an equation of the line that passes through each pair of points.

1.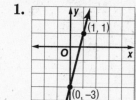

2.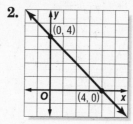

3.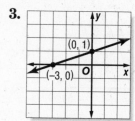

4. $(-1, 6), (7, -10)$

5. $(0, 2), (1, 7)$

6. $(6, -25), (-1, 3)$

7. $(-2, -1), (2, 11)$

8. $(10, -1), (4, 2)$

9. $(-14, -2), (7, 7)$

10. Write an equation of a line that passes through the x-intercept 4 and y-intercept −2.

11. Write an equation of a line that passes through the x-intercept −3 and y-intercept 5.

12. Write an equation of a line that passes through (0, 16) and (−10, 0).

5-4 Skills Practice

Writing Equations in Slope-Intercept Form

Write an equation of the line that passes through each point with the given slope.

1.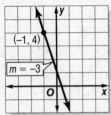

2.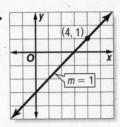

3.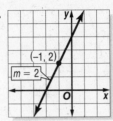

4. $(1, 9)$, $m = 4$

5. $(4, 2)$, $m = -2$

6. $(2, -2)$, $m = 3$

7. $(3, 0)$, $m = 5$

8. $(-3, -2)$, $m = 2$

9. $(-5, 4)$, $m = -4$

Write an equation of the line that passes through each pair of points.

10.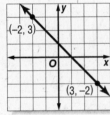

11.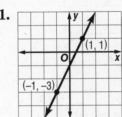

12.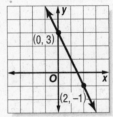

13. $(1, 3)$, $(-3, -5)$

14. $(1, 4)$, $(6, -1)$

15. $(1, -1)$, $(3, 5)$

16. $(-2, 4)$, $(0, 6)$

17. $(3, 3)$, $(1, -3)$

18. $(-1, 6)$, $(3, -2)$

Write an equation of the line that has each pair of intercepts.

19. x-intercept: -3, y-intercept: 6

20. x-intercept: 3, y-intercept: 3

21. x-intercept: 1, y-intercept: 2

22. x-intercept: 2, y-intercept: -4

23. x-intercept: -4, y-intercept: -8

24. x-intercept: -1, y-intercept: 4

Lesson 5-4

5-4 Practice

Writing Equations in Slope-Intercept Form

Write an equation of the line that passes through each point with the given slope.

1.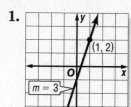

2.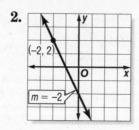

3.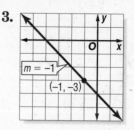

4. $(-5, 4), m = -3$

5. $(4, 3), m = \dfrac{1}{2}$

6. $(1, -5), m = -\dfrac{3}{2}$

Write an equation of the line that passes through each pair of points.

7.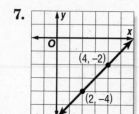

8.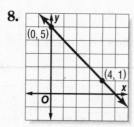

9.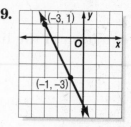

10. $(0, -4), (5, -4)$

11. $(-4, -2), (4, 0)$

12. $(-2, -3), (4, 5)$

13. $(0, 1), (5, 3)$

14. $(-3, 0), (1, -6)$

15. $(1, 0), (5, -1)$

Write an equation of the line that has each pair of intercepts.

16. x-intercept: 2, y-intercept: -5

17. x-intercept: 2, y-intercept: 10

18. x-intercept: -2, y-intercept: 1

19. x-intercept: -4, y-intercept: -3

20. DANCE LESSONS The cost for 7 dance lessons is $82. The cost for 11 lessons is $122. Write a linear equation to find the total cost C for ℓ lessons. Then use the equation to find the cost of 4 lessons.

21. WEATHER It is 76°F at the 6000-foot level of a mountain, and 49°F at the 12,000-foot level of the mountain. Write a linear equation to find the temperature T at an elevation e on the mountain, where e is in thousands of feet.

NAME _____ DATE _____ PERIOD _____

5-4 Reading to Learn Mathematics
Writing Equations in Slope-Intercept Form

Pre-Activity **How can slope-intercept form be used to make predictions?**

Read the introduction to Lesson 5-4 at the top of page 280 in your textbook.

- What is the rate of change per year?
- Study the pattern on the graph. How would you find the population in 1997?

Reading the Lesson

1. Suppose you are given that a line goes through (2, 5) and has a slope of −2. Use this information to complete the following equation.

$$y \quad = \quad \overbrace{mx} \quad + \quad b$$

$$\boxed{} = \boxed{} \cdot \boxed{} + \boxed{}$$

2. What must you first do if you are not given the slope in the problem?

3. What is the first step in answering any standardized test practice question?

4. What are four steps you can use in solving a word problem?

5. Define the term *linear extrapolation*.

Helping You Remember

6. In your own words, explain how you would answer a question that asks you to write the slope-intercept form of an equation.

© Glencoe/McGraw-Hill   **303**   Glencoe Algebra 1

5-4 Enrichment

Celsius and Kelvin Temperatures

If you blow up a balloon and put it in the refrigerator, the balloon will shrink as the temperature of the air in the balloon decreases.

The volume of a certain gas is measured at 30° Celsius. The temperature is decreased and the volume is measured again.

Temperature (t)	Volume (V)
30°C	202 mL
21°C	196 mL
0°C	182 mL
−12°C	174 mL
−27°C	164 mL

1. Graph this table on the coordinate plane provided below.

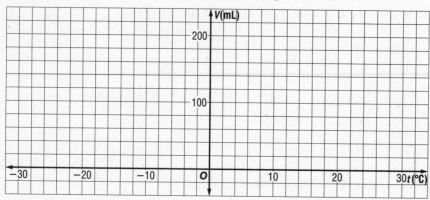

2. Find the equation of the line that passes through the points you graphed in Exercise 1.

3. Use the equation you found in Exercise 2 to find the temperature that would give a volume of zero. This temperature is the lowest one possible and is called *absolute zero*.

4. In 1848, Lord Kelvin proposed a new temperature scale with 0 being assigned to absolute zero. The size of the degree chosen was the same size as the Celsius degree. Change each of the Celsius temperatures in the table above to degrees Kelvin.

Glencoe Algebra 1

5-5 Study Guide and Intervention

Writing Equations in Point-Slope Form

Point-Slope Form

Point-Slope Form	$y - y_1 = m(x - x_1)$, where (x_1, y_1) is a given point on a nonvertical line and m is the slope of the line

Example 1 Write the point-slope form of an equation for a line that passes through (6, 1) and has a slope of $-\dfrac{5}{2}$.

$y - y_1 = m(x - x_1)$ Point-slope form

$y - 1 = -\dfrac{5}{2}(x - 6)$ $m = -\dfrac{5}{2}$; $(x_1, y_1) = (6, 1)$

Therefore, the equation is $y - 1 = -\dfrac{5}{2}(x - 6)$.

Example 2 Write the point-slope form of an equation for a horizontal line that passes through (4, −1).

$y - y_1 = m(x - x_1)$ Point-slope form

$y - (-1) = 0(x - 4)$ $m = 0$; $(x_1, y_1) = (4, -1)$

$y + 1 = 0$ Simplify.

Therefore, the equation is $y + 1 = 0$.

Exercises

Write the point-slope form of an equation for a line that passes through each point with the given slope.

1.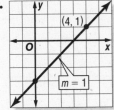

2.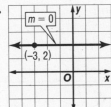

3.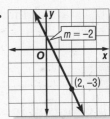

4. $(2, 1)$, $m = 4$

5. $(-7, 2)$, $m = 6$

6. $(8, 3)$, $m = 1$

7. $(-6, 7)$, $m = 0$

8. $(4, 9)$, $m = \dfrac{3}{4}$

9. $(-4, -5)$, $m = -\dfrac{1}{2}$

10. Write the point-slope form of an equation for the horizontal line that passes through $(4, -2)$.

11. Write the point-slope form of an equation for the horizontal line that passes through $(-5, 6)$.

12. Write the point-slope form of an equation for the horizontal line that passes through $(5, 0)$.

Lesson 5-5

5-5 Study Guide and Intervention (continued)
Writing Equations in Point-Slope Form

Forms of Linear Equations

Slope-Intercept Form	$y = mx + b$	m = slope; b = y-intercept
Point-Slope Form	$y - y_1 = m(x - x_1)$	m = slope; (x_1, y_1) is a given point.
Standard Form	$Ax + By = C$	A and B are not both zero. Usually A is nonnegative and A, B, and C are integers whose greatest common factor is 1.

Example 1 Write $y + 5 = \frac{2}{3}(x - 6)$ in standard form.

$$y + 5 = \frac{2}{3}(x - 6) \qquad \text{Original equation}$$

$$3(y + 5) = 3\left(\frac{2}{3}\right)(x - 6) \qquad \text{Multiply each side by 3.}$$

$$3y + 15 = 2(x - 6) \qquad \text{Distributive Property}$$
$$3y + 15 = 2x - 12 \qquad \text{Distributive Property}$$
$$3y = 2x - 27 \qquad \text{Subtract 15 from each side.}$$
$$-2x + 3y = -27 \qquad \text{Add } -2x \text{ to each side.}$$
$$2x - 3y = 27 \qquad \text{Multiply each side by } -1.$$

Therefore, the standard form of the equation is $2x - 3y = 27$.

Example 2 Write $y - 2 = -\frac{1}{4}(x - 8)$ in slope-intercept form.

$$y - 2 = -\frac{1}{4}(x - 8) \qquad \text{Original equation}$$

$$y - 2 = -\frac{1}{4}x + 2 \qquad \text{Distributive Property}$$

$$y = -\frac{1}{4}x + 4 \qquad \text{Add 2 to each side.}$$

Therefore, the slope-intercept form of the equation is $y = -\frac{1}{4}x + 4$.

Exercises

Write each equation in standard form.

1. $y + 2 = -3(x - 1)$

2. $y - 1 = -\frac{1}{3}(x - 6)$

3. $y + 2 = \frac{2}{3}(x - 9)$

4. $y + 3 = -(x - 5)$

5. $y - 4 = \frac{5}{3}(x + 3)$

6. $y + 4 = -\frac{2}{5}(x - 1)$

Write each equation in slope-intercept form.

7. $y + 4 = 4(x - 2)$

8. $y - 5 = \frac{1}{3}(x - 6)$

9. $y - 8 = -\frac{1}{4}(x + 8)$

10. $y - 6 = 3\left(x - \frac{1}{3}\right)$

11. $y + 4 = -2(x + 5)$

12. $y + \frac{5}{3} = \frac{1}{2}(x - 2)$

5-5 Skills Practice

Writing Equations in Point-Slope Form

Write the point-slope form of an equation for a line that passes through each point with the given slope.

1.
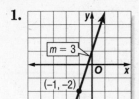

2.
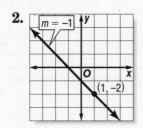

3.
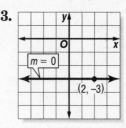

4. $(3, 1)$, $m = 0$

5. $(-4, 6)$, $m = 8$

6. $(1, -3)$, $m = -4$

7. $(4, -6)$, $m = 1$

8. $(3, 3)$, $m = \dfrac{4}{3}$

9. $(-5, -1)$, $m = -\dfrac{5}{4}$

Write each equation in standard form.

10. $y + 1 = x + 2$

11. $y + 9 = -3(x - 2)$

12. $y - 7 = 4(x + 4)$

13. $y - 4 = -(x - 1)$

14. $y - 6 = 4(x + 3)$

15. $y + 5 = -5(x - 3)$

16. $y - 10 = -2(x - 3)$

17. $y - 2 = -\dfrac{1}{2}(x - 4)$

18. $y + 11 = \dfrac{1}{3}(x + 3)$

Write each equation in slope-intercept form.

19. $y - 4 = 3(x - 2)$

20. $y + 2 = -(x + 4)$

21. $y - 6 = -2(x + 2)$

22. $y + 1 = -5(x - 3)$

23. $y - 3 = 6(x - 1)$

24. $y - 8 = 3(x + 5)$

25. $y - 2 = \dfrac{1}{2}(x + 6)$

26. $y + 1 = -\dfrac{1}{3}(x + 9)$

27. $y - \dfrac{1}{2} = x + \dfrac{1}{2}$

Lesson 5-5

NAME _____ DATE _____ PERIOD _____

Practice

Writing Equations in Point-Slope Form

Write the point-slope form of an equation for a line that passes through each point with the given slope.

1. $(2, 2)$, $m = -3$

2. $(1, -6)$, $m = -1$

3. $(-3, -4)$, $m = 0$

4. $(1, 3)$, $m = -\dfrac{3}{4}$

5. $(-8, 5)$, $m = -\dfrac{2}{5}$

6. $(3, -3)$, $m = \dfrac{1}{3}$

Write each equation in standard form.

7. $y - 11 = 3(x - 2)$

8. $y - 10 = -(x - 2)$

9. $y + 7 = 2(x + 5)$

10. $y - 5 = \dfrac{3}{2}(x + 4)$

11. $y + 2 = -\dfrac{3}{4}(x + 1)$

12. $y - 6 = \dfrac{4}{3}(x - 3)$

13. $y + 4 = 1.5(x + 2)$

14. $y - 3 = -2.4(x - 5)$

15. $y - 4 = 2.5(x + 3)$

Write each equation in slope-intercept form.

16. $y + 2 = 4(x + 2)$

17. $y + 1 = -7(x + 1)$

18. $y - 3 = -5(x + 12)$

19. $y - 5 = \dfrac{3}{2}(x + 4)$

20. $y - \dfrac{1}{4} = -3\left(x + \dfrac{1}{4}\right)$

21. $y - \dfrac{2}{3} = -2\left(x - \dfrac{1}{4}\right)$

CONSTRUCTION For Exercises 22–24, use the following information.

A construction company charges $15 per hour for debris removal, plus a one-time fee for the use of a trash dumpster. The total fee for 9 hours of service is $195.

22. Write the point-slope form of an equation to find the total fee y for any number of hours x.

23. Write the equation in slope-intercept form.

24. What is the fee for the use of a trash dumpster?

MOVING For Exercises 25–27, use the following information.

There is a set daily fee for renting a moving truck, plus a charge of $0.50 per mile driven. It costs $64 to rent the truck on a day when it is driven 48 miles.

25. Write the point-slope form of an equation to find the total charge y for any number of miles x for a one-day rental.

26. Write the equation in slope-intercept form.

27. What is the daily fee?

5-5 Reading to Learn Mathematics

Writing Equations in Point-Slope Form

Pre-Activity **How can you use the slope formula to write an equation of a line?**

Read the introduction to Lesson 5-5 at the top of page 286 in your textbook.

Note that in the final equation there is a value subtracted from x and from y. What are these values?

Reading the Lesson

1. In the formula $y - y_1 = m(x - x_1)$, what do x_1 and y_1 represent?

2. Complete the chart below by listing three forms of equations. Then write the formula for each form. Finally, write three examples of equations in those forms.

Form of Equation	Formula	Example

3. Refer to Example 5 on page 288 of your textbook. What do you think the *hypotenuse* of a right triangle is?

Helping You Remember

4. Suppose you could not remember all three formulas listed in the table above. Which of the forms would you concentrate on for writing linear equations? Explain why you chose that form.

Lesson 5-5

5-5 **Enrichment**

Collinearity

You have learned how to find the slope between two points on a line. Does it matter which two points you use? How does your choice of points affect the slope-intercept form of the equation of the line?

1. Choose three different pairs of points from the graph at the right. Write the slope-intercept form of the line using each pair.

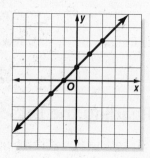

2. How are the equations related?

3. What conclusion can you draw from your answers to Exercises 1 and 2?

When points are contained in the same line, they are said to be **collinear**. Even though points may *look* like they form a straight line when connected, it does not mean that they actually do. By checking pairs of points on a line you can determine whether the line represents a linear relationship.

4. Choose several pairs of points from the graph at the right and write the slope-intercept form of the line using each pair.

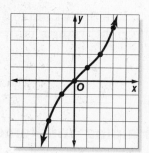

5. What conclusion can you draw from your equations in Exercise 4? Is this a straight line?

5-6

Study Guide and Intervention

Geometry: Parallel and Perpendicular Lines

Parallel Lines Two nonvertical lines are **parallel** if they have the same slope. All vertical lines are parallel.

Example Write the slope-intercept form for an equation of the line that passes through $(-1, 6)$ and is parallel to the graph of $y = 2x + 12$.

A line parallel to $y = 2x + 12$ has the same slope, 2. Replace m with 2 and (x_1, y_1) with $(-1, 6)$ in the point-slope form.

$y - y_1 = m(x - x_1)$	Point-slope form
$y - 6 = 2(x - (-1))$	$m = 2; (x_1, y_1) = (-1, 6)$
$y - 6 = 2(x + 1)$	Simplify.
$y - 6 = 2x + 2$	Distributive Property
$y = 2x + 8$	Slope-intercept form

Therefore, the equation is $y = 2x + 8$.

Exercises

Write the slope-intercept form for an equation of the line that passes through the given point and is parallel to the graph of each equation.

1.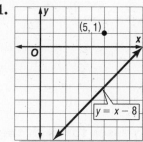

2.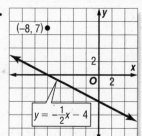

3.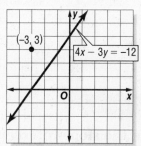

4. $(-2, 2), y = 4x - 2$

5. $(6, 4), y = \dfrac{1}{3}x + 1$

6. $(4, -2), y = -2x + 3$

7. $(-2, 4), y = -3x + 10$

8. $(-1, 6), 3x + y = 12$

9. $(4, -6), x + 2y = 5$

10. Find an equation of the line that has a y-intercept of 2 that is parallel to the graph of the line $4x + 2y = 8$.

11. Find an equation of the line that has a y-intercept of -1 that is parallel to the graph of the line $x - 3y = 6$.

12. Find an equation of the line that has a y-intercept of -4 that is parallel to the graph of the line $y = 6$.

5-6 Study Guide and Intervention *(continued)*

Geometry: Parallel and Perpendicular Lines

Perpendicular Lines Two lines are **perpendicular** if their slopes are negative reciprocals of each other. Vertical and horizontal lines are perpendicular.

Example Write the slope-intercept form for an equation that passes through $(-4, 2)$ and is perpendicular to the graph of $2x - 3y = 9$.

Find the slope of $2x - 3y = 9$.

$2x - 3y = 9$	Original equation
$-3y = -2x + 9$	Subtract 2x from each side.
$y = \dfrac{2}{3}x - 3$	Divide each side by −3.

The slope of $y = \dfrac{2}{3}x - 3$ is $\dfrac{2}{3}$. So, the slope of the line passing through $(-4, 2)$ that is perpendicular to this line is the negative reciprocal of $\dfrac{2}{3}$, or $-\dfrac{3}{2}$.
Use the point-slope form to find the equation.

$y - y_1 = m(x - x_1)$	Point-slope form
$y - 2 = -\dfrac{3}{2}(x - (-4))$	$m = -\dfrac{3}{2}; (x_1, y_1) = (-4, 2)$
$y - 2 = -\dfrac{3}{2}(x + 4)$	Simplify.
$y - 2 = -\dfrac{3}{2}x - 6$	Distributive Property
$y = -\dfrac{3}{2}x - 4$	Slope-intercept form

Exercises

Write the slope-intercept form for an equation of the line that passes through the given point and is perpendicular to the graph of each equation.

1. $(4, 2), y = \dfrac{1}{2}x + 1$ **2.** $(2, -3), y = -\dfrac{2}{3}x + 4$ **3.** $(6, 4), y = 7x + 1$

4. $(-8, -7), y = -x - 8$ **5.** $(6, -2), y = -3x - 6$ **6.** $(-5, -1), y = \dfrac{5}{2}x - 3$

7. $(-9, -5), y = -3x - 1$ **8.** $(-1, 3), 2x + 4y = 12$ **9.** $(6, -6), 3x - y = 6$

10. Find an equation of the line that has a y-intercept of -2 and is perpendicular to the graph of the line $x - 2y = 5$.

11. Find an equation of the line that has a y-intercept of 5 and is perpendicular to the graph of the line $4x + 3y = 8$.

5-6 Skills Practice

Geometry: Parallel and Perpendicular Lines

Write the slope-intercept form of an equation of the line that passes through the given point and is parallel to the graph of each equation.

1.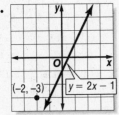

2.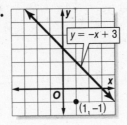

3.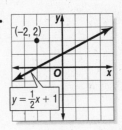

4. $(3, 2), y = 3x + 4$

5. $(-1, -2), y = -3x + 5$

6. $(-1, 1), y = x - 4$

7. $(1, -3), y = -4x - 1$

8. $(-4, 2), y = x + 3$

9. $(-4, 3), y = \frac{1}{2}x - 6$

10. $(4, 1), y = -\frac{1}{4}x + 7$

11. $(-5, -1), 2y = 2x - 4$

12. $(3, -1), 3y = x + 9$

Write the slope-intercept form of an equation of the line that passes through the given point and is perpendicular to the graph of each equation.

13. $(-3, -2), y = x + 2$

14. $(4, -1), y = 2x - 4$

15. $(-1, -6), x + 3y = 6$

16. $(-4, 5), y = -4x - 1$

17. $(-2, 3), y = \frac{1}{4}x - 4$

18. $(0, 0), y = \frac{1}{2}x - 1$

19. $(3, -3), y = \frac{3}{4}x + 5$

20. $(-5, 1), y = -\frac{5}{3}x - 7$

21. $(0, -2), y = -7x + 3$

22. $(2, 3), 2x + 10y = 3$

23. $(-2, 2), 6x + 3y = -9$

24. $(-4, -3), 8x - 2y = 16$

5-6 Practice

Geometry: Parallel and Perpendicular Lines

Write the slope-intercept form of an equation of the line that passes through the given point and is parallel to the graph of each equation.

1. $(3, 2), y = x + 5$

2. $(-2, 5), y = -4x + 2$

3. $(4, -6), y = -\dfrac{3}{4}x + 1$

4. $(5, 4), y = \dfrac{2}{5}x - 2$

5. $(12, 3), y = \dfrac{4}{3}x + 5$

6. $(3, 1), 2x + y = 5$

7. $(-3, 4), 3y = 2x - 3$

8. $(-1, -2), 3x - y = 5$

9. $(-8, 2), 5x - 4y = 1$

10. $(-1, -4), 9x + 3y = 8$

11. $(-5, 6), 4x + 3y = 1$

12. $(3, 1), 2x + 5y = 7$

Write the slope-intercept form of an equation of the line that passes through the given point and is perpendicular to the graph of each equation.

13. $(-2, -2), y = -\dfrac{1}{3}x + 9$

14. $(-6, 5), x - y = 5$

15. $(-4, -3), 4x + y = 7$

16. $(0, 1), x + 5y = 15$

17. $(2, 4), x - 6y = 2$

18. $(-1, -7), 3x + 12y = -6$

19. $(-4, 1), 4x + 7y = 6$

20. $(10, 5), 5x + 4y = 8$

21. $(4, -5), 2x - 5y = -10$

22. $(1, 1), 3x + 2y = -7$

23. $(-6, -5), 4x + 3y = -6$

24. $(-3, 5), 5x - 6y = 9$

25. **GEOMETRY** Quadrilateral $ABCD$ has diagonals $\overline{AC}$ and $\overline{BD}$. Determine whether $\overline{AC}$ is perpendicular to $\overline{BD}$. Explain.

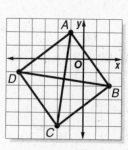

26. **GEOMETRY** Triangle ABC has vertices $A(0, 4)$, $B(1, 2)$, and $C(4, 6)$. Determine whether triangle ABC is a right triangle. Explain.

5-6 Reading to Learn Mathematics

Geometry: Parallel and Perpendicular Lines

Pre-Activity **How can you determine whether two lines are parallel?**

Read the introduction to Lesson 5-6 at the top of page 292 in your textbook.

• What is a family of graphs?

• Do you think lines that do not appear to intersect are parallel or perpendicular?

Reading the Lesson

1. Refer to the Key Concept box on page 292. Why does the definition use the term *nonvertical* when talking about lines with the same slope?

2. What is a right angle?

3. Refer to the Key Concept box on page 293. Describe how you find the opposite reciprocal of a number.

4. Write the opposite reciprocal of each number.

   a. 2 　　　　　　　 **b.** −3 　　　　　　 **c.** $\frac{12}{13}$ 　　　　　 **d.** $-\frac{1}{5}$

Helping You Remember

5. One way to remember how slopes of parallel lines are related is to say "same direction, same slope." Try to think of a phrase to help you remember that perpendicular lines have slopes that are opposite reciprocals.

5-6 Enrichment

Pencils of Lines

All of the lines that pass through a single point in the same plane are called a **pencil of lines**.

All lines with the same slope, but different intercepts, are also called a "pencil," a **pencil of parallel lines**.

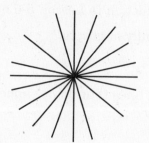 

Graph some of the lines in each pencil.

1. A pencil of lines through the point (1, 3)

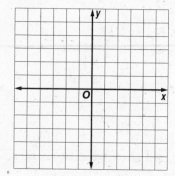

2. A pencil of lines described by $y - 4 = m(x - 2)$, where m is any real number

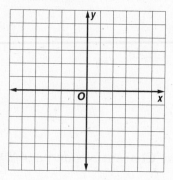

3. A pencil of lines parallel to the line $x - 2y = 7$

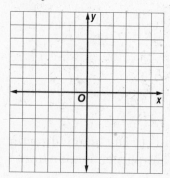

4. A pencil of lines described by $y = mx + 3m - 2$

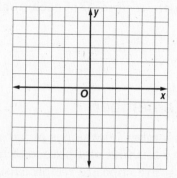

5-7 Study Guide and Intervention

Scatter Plots and Lines of Fit

Interpret Points on a Scatter Plot A **scatter plot** is a graph in which two sets of data are plotted as ordered pairs in a coordinate plane. If y increases as x increases, there is a **positive correlation** between x and y. If y decreases as x increases, there is a **negative correlation** between x and y. If x and y are not related, there is **no correlation**.

Example EARNINGS The graph at the right shows the amount of money Carmen earned each week and the amount she deposited in her savings account that same week. Determine whether the graph shows a positive correlation, a negative correlation, or no correlation. If there is a positive or negative correlation, describe its meaning in the situation.

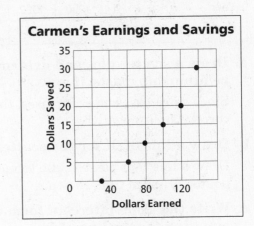

The graph shows a positive correlation. The more Carmen earns, the more she saves.

Exercises

Determine whether each graph shows a positive correlation, a negative correlation, or no correlation. If there is a positive correlation, describe it.

1.
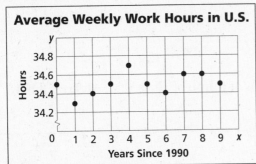

Source: *The World Almanac*

2.
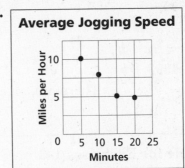

3.
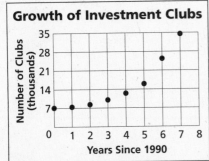

Source: *The Wall Street Journal Almanac*

4.
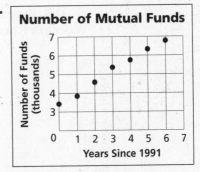

Source: *The Wall Street Journal Almanac*

Lesson 5-7

5-7 Study Guide and Intervention (continued)

Scatter Plots and Lines of Fit

Lines of Fit

Example The table below shows the number of students per computer in United States public schools for certain school years from 1990 to 2000.

Year	1990	1992	1994	1996	1998	2000
Students per Computer	22	18	14	10	6.1	5.4

a. Draw a scatter plot and determine what relationship exists, if any.

Since y decreases as x increases, the correlation is negative.

b. Draw a line of fit for the scatter plot.

Draw a line that passes close to most of the points. A line of fit is shown.

c. Write the slope-intercept form of an equation for the line of fit.

The line of fit shown passes through (1993, 16) and (1999, 5.7). Find the slope.

$$m = \frac{5.7 - 16}{1999 - 1993}$$

$$m = -1.7$$

Find b in $y = -1.7x + b$.

$$16 = -1.7 \cdot 1993 + b$$

$$3404 = b$$

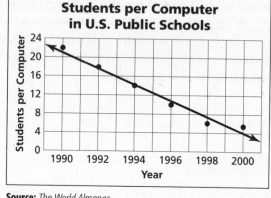

Students per Computer in U.S. Public Schools

Source: *The World Almanac*

Therefore, an equation of a line of fit is $y = -1.7x + 3404$.

Exercises

Refer to the table for Exercises 1–3.

Years Since 1995	Hourly Wage
0	$11.43
1	$11.82
2	$12.28
3	$12.78
4	$13.24

1. Draw a scatter plot.

2. Draw a line of fit for the data.

3. Write the slope-intercept form of an equation for the line of fit.

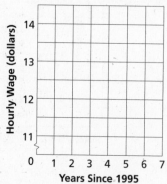

U.S. Production Workers Hourly Wage

Source: *The World Almanac*

Glencoe Algebra 1

5-7 Skills Practice

Statistics: Scatter Plots and Lines of Fit

Determine whether each graph shows a *positive correlation*, a *negative correlation*, or *no correlation*. If there is a positive or negative correlation, describe its meaning in the situation.

1.

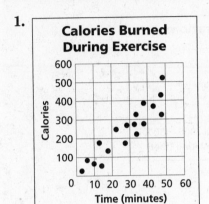

2.

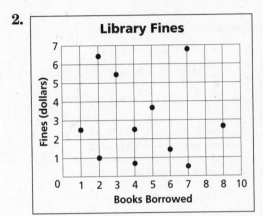

3.

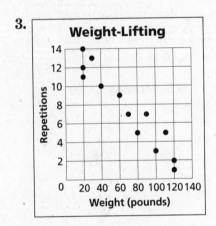

4.

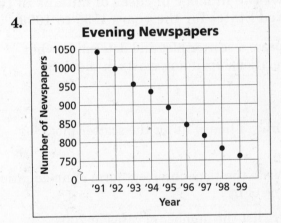

Source: Editor & Publisher

BASEBALL For Exercises 5–7, use the scatter plot that shows the average price of a major-league baseball ticket from 1991 to 2000.

5. Determine what relationship, if any, exists in the data. Explain.

6. Use the points (1993, 9.60) and (1998, 13.60) to write the slope-intercept form of an equation for the line of fit shown in the scatter plot.

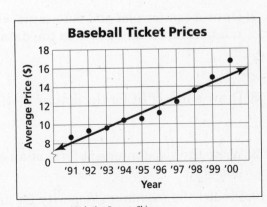

Source: Team Marketing Report, Chicago

7. Predict the price of a ticket in 2004.

5-7 Practice

Statistics: Scatter Plots and Lines of Fit

Determine whether each graph shows a *positive correlation*, a *negative correlation*, or *no correlation*. If there is a positive or negative correlation, describe its meaning in the situation.

1.
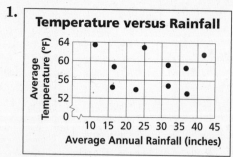

Source: National Oceanic and Atmospheric Administration

2.
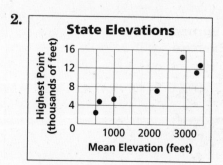

Source: U.S. Geological Survey

DISEASE For Exercises 3–6, use the table that shows the number of cases of mumps in the United States for the years 1995 to 1999.

U.S. Mumps Cases					
Year	1995	1996	1997	1998	1999
Cases	906	751	683	666	387

Source: Centers for Disease Control and Prevention

3. Draw a scatter plot and determine what relationship, if any, exists in the data.

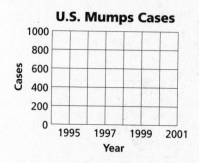

4. Draw a line of fit for the scatter plot.

5. Write the slope-intercept form of an equation for the line of fit.

6. Predict the number of cases in 2004.

ZOOS For Exercises 7–10, use the table that shows the average and maximum longevity of various animals in captivity.

Longevity (years)								
Avg.	12	25	15	8	35	40	41	20
Max.	47	50	40	20	70	77	61	54

Source: Walker's Mammals of the World

7. Draw a scatter plot and determine what relationship, if any, exists in the data.

8. Draw a line of fit for the scatter plot.

9. Write the slope-intercept form of an equation for the line of fit.

10. Predict the maximum longevity for an animal with an average longevity of 33 years.

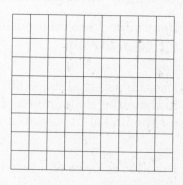

Glencoe Algebra 1

5-7 Reading to Learn Mathematics

Statistics: Scatter Plots and Lines of Fit

Lesson 5-7

Pre-Activity **How do scatter plots help identify trends in data?**

Read the introduction to Lesson 5-7 at the top of page 298 in your textbook.

• What does the phrase *linear relationship* mean to you?

• Write three ordered pairs that fit the description *as x increases, y decreases*.

Reading the Lesson

1. Look up the word *scatter* in a dictionary. How does this definition compare to the term *scatter plot*?

2. What is a *line of fit*? How many data points fall on the line of fit?

3. What is *linear interpolation*? How can you distinguish it from linear *extrapolation*?

Helping You Remember

4. How can you remember whether a set of data points shows a positive correlation or a negative correlation?

5-7 Enrichment

Latitude and Temperature

The *latitude* of a place on Earth is the measure of its distance from the equator. What do you think is the relationship between a city's latitude and its January temperature? At the right is a table containing the latitudes and January mean temperatures for fifteen U.S. cities.

U.S. City	Latitude	January Mean Temperature
Albany, New York	42:40 N	20.7°F
Albuquerque, New Mexico	35:07 N	34.3°F
Anchorage, Alaska	61:11 N	14.9°F
Birmingham, Alabama	33:32 N	41.7°F
Charleston, South Carolina	32:47 N	47.1°F
Chicago, Illinois	41:50 N	21.0°F
Columbus, Ohio	39:59 N	26.3°F
Duluth, Minnesota	46:47 N	7.0°F
Fairbanks, Alaska	64:50 N	−10.1°F
Galveston, Texas	29:14 N	52.9°F
Honolulu, Hawaii	21:19 N	72.9°F
Las Vegas, Nevada	36:12 N	45.1°F
Miami, Florida	25:47 N	67.3°F
Richmond, Virginia	37:32 N	35.8°F
Tucson, Arizona	32:12 N	51.3°F

Sources: www.indo.com and www.nws.noaa.gov/climatex.html

1. Use the information in the table to create a scatter plot and draw a line of best fit for the data.

2. Write an equation for the line of fit. Make a conjecture about the relationship between a city's latitude and its mean January temperature.

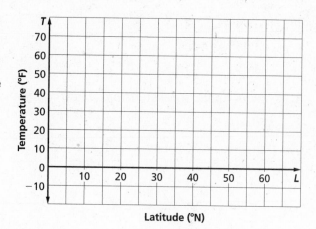

Latitude (°N)

3. Use your equation to predict the January mean temperature of Juneau, Alaska, which has latitude 58:23 N.

4. What would you expect to be the latitude of a city with a January mean temperature of 15°F?

5. Was your conjecture about the relationship between latitude and temperature correct?

6. Research the latitudes and temperatures for cities in the southern hemisphere instead. Does your conjecture hold for these cities as well?

5) Chapter 5 Test, Form 1

SCORE _____

Write the letter for the correct answer in the blank at the right of each question.

For Questions 1–4, find the slope of each line described.

1. the line through $(3, 7)$ and $(-1, 4)$

   A. $\frac{4}{3}$ **B.** $\frac{3}{4}$ **C.** $\frac{11}{2}$ **D.** $\frac{2}{11}$ 1. _____

2. the line through $(-3, 2)$ and $(6, 2)$

   A. $\frac{4}{9}$ **B.** $\frac{4}{3}$ **C.** 0 **D.** undefined 2. _____

3. the line graphed at the right

   A. $\frac{2}{3}$ **B.** $\frac{3}{2}$
   C. $-\frac{3}{2}$ **D.** $-\frac{2}{3}$

   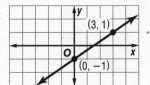

   3. _____

4. a vertical line

   A. 1 **B.** 0 **C.** -1 **D.** undefined 4. _____

5. Which graph has a slope of -3?

   A.   **B.**   **C.**   **D.**   5. _____

6. **COMMUNICATION** In 1996, there were 171 area codes in the United States. In 1999, there were 285. Find the rate of change from 1996 to 1999.

   A. 114 **B.** 38 **C.** $\frac{1}{38}$ **D.** -144 6. _____

For Questions 7–9, find the equation in slope-intercept form that describes each line.

7. a line through $(2, 4)$ with slope 0

   A. $y = 2$ **B.** $x = 2$ **C.** $y = 4$ **D.** $x = 4$ 7. _____

8. a line through $(4, 2)$ with slope $\frac{1}{2}$

   A. $y = -\frac{1}{2}x$ **B.** $y = \frac{1}{2}x - 4$ **C.** $y = 2x - 10$ **D.** $y = \frac{1}{2}x$ 8. _____

9. a line through $(-1, 1)$ and $(2, 3)$

   A. $y = \frac{2}{3}x + \frac{5}{3}$ **B.** $y = -\frac{2}{3}x + \frac{5}{3}$ **C.** $y = \frac{2}{3}x - \frac{5}{3}$ **D.** $y = -\frac{2}{3}x - \frac{5}{3}$ 9. _____

10. If 5 deli sandwiches cost \$29.75, how much will 8 sandwiches cost?

    A. \$37.75 **B.** \$29.75 **C.** \$47.60 **D.** \$0.16 10. _____

11. What is the standard form of $y - 8 = 2(x + 3)$?

    A. $2x + y = 14$ **B.** $y = 2x + 14$ **C.** $2x - y = -14$ **D.** $y - 2x = 11$ 11. _____

Assessment

12. Which is the graph of $y = -\frac{3}{4}x$?

A. **B.** **C.** **D.**

12. _____

13. Which is the point-slope form of an equation for the line that passes through $(0, -5)$ with slope 2?

A. $y = 2x - 5$ **B.** $y + 5 = 2x$ **C.** $y - 5 = x - 2$ **D.** $y = 2(x + 5)$ **13.** _____

14. What is the slope-intercept form of $y + 6 = 2(x + 2)$?

A. $y = 2x - 6$ **B.** $y = 2x - 2$ **C.** $y = 2x + 6$ **D.** $2x - y = 6$ **14.** _____

15. When are two lines parallel?

A. when the slopes are opposite   **B.** when the slopes are equal

C. when the product of the slopes is 1   **D.** when the slopes are positive   **15.** _____

16. Find the slope-intercept form of an equation for the line that passes through $(-1, 2)$ and is parallel to $y = 2x - 3$.

A. $y = 2x + 4$ **B.** $y = 0.5x + 4$ **C.** $y = 2x + 3$ **D.** $y = -0.5x - 4$ **16.** _____

17. Find the slope-intercept form of an equation of the line perpendicular to the graph of $x - 3y = 5$ and passing through $(0, 6)$.

A. $y = \frac{1}{3}x - 2$ **B.** $y = -3x + 6$ **C.** $y = \frac{1}{3}x + 2$ **D.** $y = 3x - 6$ **17.** _____

For Questions 18 and 19, use the scatter plot at the right.

18. How would you describe the relationship between the x and y values in the scatter plot?

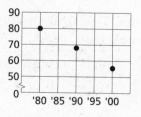

A. strong negative correlation

B. weak negative correlation

C. weak positive correlation

D. strong positive correlation   **18.** _____

19. Based on the data in the scatter plot, what would you expect the y value to be for $x = 2010$?

A. greater than 80   **B.** between 80 and 65

C. between 65 and 50   **D.** less than 50   **19.** _____

20. What is an equation of the line whose graph has slope of 2 and a y-intercept of -5?

A. $y = -5x + 2$ **B.** $y = 5x + 2$ **C.** $y = 2x + 5$ **D.** $y = 2x - 5$ **20.** _____

Bonus Find the value of r in $(4, r)$, $(r, 2)$ so that the slope of the line containing them is $-\frac{5}{3}$.

B: _____

5 | # Chapter 5 Test, Form 2A

SCORE _____

Write the letter for the correct answer in the blank at the right of each question.

1. What is the slope of the line through $(1, 9)$ and $(-3, 16)$?

   A. $-\dfrac{7}{4}$ **B.** $-\dfrac{4}{7}$ **C.** $-\dfrac{25}{2}$ **D.** $-\dfrac{2}{25}$

   1. _____

2. What is the slope of the line through $(-4, 3)$ and $(5, 3)$?

   A. 0 **B.** undefined **C.** 9 **D.** 1

   2. _____

3. Find the value of r so that the line through $(8, r)$ and $(4, 5)$ has a slope of -4.

   A. 11 **B.** -11 **C.** 4 **D.** -4

   3. _____

4. In 1995, there were 12,000 students at Beacon High. In 2000, there were 12,250. What is the rate of change in the number of students?

   A. 250/yr **B.** 50/yr **C.** 42/yr **D.** 200/yr

   4. _____

5. Which is the graph of $y = \dfrac{2}{3}x$?

   A.   **B.**   **C.**   **D.**

   5. _____

 skip

6. If y varies directly as x and $y = 3$ when $x = 10$, find x when $y = 8$.

   A. $\dfrac{80}{3}$ **B.** $\dfrac{12}{5}$ **C.** $\dfrac{15}{4}$ **D.** none of these

   6. *skip* _____

7. A driver's distance varies directly as the amount of time traveled. After 6 hours, a driver had traveled 390 miles. How far had the driver traveled after 4 hours?

   A. 130 miles **B.** 220 miles **C.** 260 miles **D.** 650 miles

   7. _____

8. A line of fit might be defined as

   A. a line that connects all the data points.
   B. a line that might best estimate the data and be used for predicting values.
   C. a vertical line halfway through the data.
   D. a line whose slope is greater than 1.

   8. _____

9. What is the slope-intercept form of the equation of a line with slope 5 and y-intercept -8?

   A. $y = -8x + 5$ **B.** $y = 8x - 5$ **C.** $5x - y = -8$ **D.** $y = 5x - 8$

   9. _____

10. Which equation is graphed at the right?

    A. $2y - x = 10$ **B.** $2x + y = -5$
    C. $2x - y = 5$ **D.** $2y + x = -5$

    10. _____

11. Which is an equation of the line that passes through $(2, -5)$ and $(6, 3)$?

    A. $y = \dfrac{1}{2}x - 6$ **B.** $y = \dfrac{1}{2}x$
    C. $y = 2x + 12$ **D.** $y = 2x - 9$

    11. _____

Assessment

12. What is the standard form of the equation of the line through $(0, -3)$ with slope $\frac{2}{5}$?

   A. $-5x + 2y = 15$

   C. $2x - 5y = 15$

   B. $-5x - 2y = -15$

   D. $-2x + 5y = 15$

   12. _____

13. Which is an equation of the line with slope -3 and a y-intercept of 5?

   A. $y = -3(x + 5)$ **B.** $y - 5 = -3x$ **C.** $-3x + y = 5$ **D.** $y = 5x - 3$

   13. _____

14. What is the standard form of $y - 7 = -\frac{2}{3}(x + 1)$?

   A. $-2x + 3y = 23$ **B.** $-3x + 2y = 17$ **C.** $2x + 3y = 19$ **D.** $3x + 2y = 11$ 14. _____

15. What is the equation of the line through $(-2, -3)$ with a slope of 0?

   A. $x = -2$ **B.** $y = -3$ **C.** $-2x - 3y = 0$ **D.** $-3x + 2y = 0$ 15. _____

16. Find the slope-intercept form of the equation of the line that passes through $(-5, 3)$ and is parallel to $12x - 3y = 10$.

   A. $y = -4x - 17$ **B.** $y = 4x - 13$ **C.** $y = -4x + 13$ **D.** $y = 4x + 23$ 16. _____

17. If line q has a slope of $-\frac{3}{8}$, what is the slope of any line perpendicular to q?

   A. $-\frac{3}{8}$ **B.** $\frac{3}{8}$ **C.** $\frac{8}{3}$ **D.** $-\frac{8}{3}$ 17. _____

For Questions 18 and 19, use the scatter plot at the right.

18. Which data are shown by the scatter plot?

   A. (1980, 5.5), (1982, 6.1), (1989, 7.6)

   B. (1980, 5.5), (1985, 6.1), (1989, 7.6)

   C. (1980, 5.5), (1985, 6.6), (1990, 8.0)

   D. (1980, 5.5), (1982, 6.6), (1990, 8.0)

   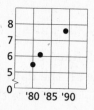

   18. _____

19. Based on the data in the scatter plot, what would you expect the y value to be for $x = 1995$?

   A. between 7 and 8

   C. between 5 and 7

   B. higher than 8

   D. impossible to tell

   19. _____

20. To calculate the charge for a load of bricks, including delivery, the Redstone Brick Co. uses the equation $C = 0.42b + 25$, where C is the charge and b is the number of bricks. What is the delivery fee per load?

   A. $42

   C. $25

   B. $67

   D. It depends on the number of bricks

   20. _____

Bonus What is the y-intercept of a line through $(2, 7)$ and perpendicular to the line $y = -\frac{3}{2}x + 6$?   **B:** _____

5 **Chapter 5 Test, Form 2B**

Write the letter for the correct answer in the blank at the right of each question.

1. What is the slope of the line through $(2, -8)$ and $(4, 1)$?

   A. $-\frac{2}{9}$ **B.** $-\frac{6}{7}$ **C.** $-\frac{7}{6}$ **D.** $\frac{9}{2}$

   1. _____

2. What is the slope of the line through $(-4, -6)$ and $(9, -6)$?

   A. $-\frac{12}{5}$ **B.** $-\frac{5}{12}$ **C.** 0 **D.** undefined

   2. _____

3. Find the value of r so that the line through $(8, 5)$ and $(4, r)$ has a slope of -4.

   A. 21 **B.** -21 **C.** 11 **D.** -11

   3. _____

4. In 1995, MusicMart sold 12,000 CDs. In 2000, they sold 14,550 CDs. What is the rate of change in the number of CDs sold?

   A. 2550/yr **B.** 510/yr **C.** 425/yr **D.** 2400/yr

   4. _____

5. Which is the graph of $y = -\frac{1}{2}x$?

   A.   **B.**   **C.**   **D.**

   5. _____

 6. If y varies directly as x and $y = 5$ when $x = 8$, find y when $x = 9$.

   A. $\frac{72}{5}$ **B.** $\frac{45}{8}$ **C.** $\frac{40}{9}$ **D.** 6

   6. _skip_

7. The amount a spring stretches varies directly as the weight of the object attached to it. If an 8-ounce weight stretches a spring 10 centimeters, how much weight will stretch it 15 centimeters?

   A. 16 oz **B.** 6 oz **C.** 10 oz **D.** 12 oz

   7. _____

8. The graph of data that has a strong negative correlation has

   A. a narrow linear pattern from lower left to upper right.

   B. a narrow linear pattern from upper left to lower right.

   C. a narrow horizontal pattern below the x-axis.

   D. all negative x-values.

   8. _____

9. What is the slope-intercept form of the equation of the line with slope $\frac{1}{4}$ and y-intercept at the origin?

   A. $y = 4x$ **B.** $y = \frac{1}{4}x$ **C.** $y = x + \frac{1}{4}$ **D.** $y + \frac{1}{4} = x$

   9. _____

10. Which equation is graphed at the right?

    A. $y - 2x = -4$ **B.** $2x + y = -4$

    C. $2x + y = 4$ **D.** $y - 4 = 2x$

    10. _____

11. Which is an equation of the line that passes through $(4, -5)$ and $(6, -9)$?

    A. $y = \frac{1}{2}x - 3$ **B.** $y = \frac{1}{2}x + 3$ **C.** $y = -2x + 3$ **D.** $y = 2x - 3$

    11. _____

5 **Chapter 5 Test, Form 2B** *(continued)*

12. What is the standard form of the equation of the line through (6, −3) with slope $\frac{2}{3}$?

    A. −2x + 3y = 24   **B.** 2x − 3y = 21   **C.** 3x − 2y = 24   **D.** 3x − 2y = −21   **12.** _____

13. Which is an equation of the line with slope −3 that passes through (2, 4)?

    A. y − 4 = −3(x − 2)   **B.** y − 4 = −3x − 2

    C. y + 4 = −3(x + 2)   **D.** y − 2 = −3(x − 4)   **13.** _____

14. What is the standard form of $y + 2 = \frac{1}{2}(x - 4)$?

    A. x + 2y = 0   **B.** x − 2y = 8   **C.** 2x − y = 10   **D.** 4x − 2y = 0   **14.** _____

15. What is the equation of the line through (−2, −3) with an undefined slope?

    A. x = −2   **B.** y = −3   **C.** −2x − 3y = 0   **D.** −3x + 2y = 0   **15.** _____

16. Find the slope-intercept form of the equation of the line that passes through (−1, 5) and is parallel to 4x + 2y = 8.

    A. y = −2x + 9   **B.** y = 2x − 9   **C.** y = 4x − 9   **D.** y = −2x + 3   **16.** _____

17. If line q has a slope of −2, what is the slope of any line perpendicular to q?

    A. 2   **B.** −2   **C.** $\frac{1}{2}$ **D.** $-\frac{1}{2}$ **17.** _____

For Questions 18 and 19, use the scatter plot at the right.

18. Which data are shown by the scatter plot?

    A. (1970, 47), (1980, 31), (1986, 24)

    B. (1970, 50), (1985, 25), (1990, 0)

    C. (47, 1970), (31, 1980), (24, 1986)

    D. (1976, 45), (1980, 35), (1985, 8)   **18.** _____

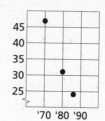

19. Based on the data in the scatter plot, which statement is true?

    A. As x increases, y increases.

    B. As x increases, y decreases.

    C. There is no relationship between x and y.

    D. There are not enough data to determine the relationship between x and y.   **19.** _____

20. A baby blue whale weighed 3 tons at birth. Ten days later, it weighed 4 tons. Assuming the same rate of growth, which equation shows the weight w when the whale is d days old?

    A. w = 10d + 3   **B.** w = 10d + 4   **C.** w = 0.1d + 3   **D.** w = d + 10   **20.** _____

Bonus For what value of k does kx + 7y = 10 have a slope of 3?   **B:** _____

5 Chapter 5 Test, Form 2C

SCORE _____

For Questions 1–3, find the slope of the line passing through each pair of points. If the slope is undefined, write "undefined."

1. $(2, 5)$ and $(3, 6)$

1. _____

2. $(-1, 3)$ and $(6, 3)$

2. _____

3. $(6, -4)$ and $(-3, 7)$

3. _____

4. Find the value of r so that the line through $(-4, 8)$ and $(r, -6)$ has a slope of $\frac{2}{3}$.

4. _____

5. In 1968, vehicle emission standards allowed 6.3 hydrocarbons released per mile driven. By 1980, the standards allowed only 0.41 hydrocarbons per mile driven. What was the rate of change from 1968 to 1980?

5. _____

6. Graph $y = -\frac{1}{2}x$.

6.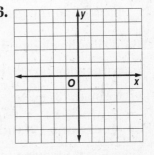

7. If a shark can swim 27 miles in 9 hours, how many miles will it swim in 12 hours?

7. _____

8. Write a linear equation in slope-intercept form to model the situation: A telephone company charges \$28.75 per month plus 10¢ a minute for long-distance calls.

8. _____

9. Write an equation in standard form of the line that passes through $(7, -3)$ and has a y-intercept of 2.

9. _____

10. Write the slope-intercept form of an equation for the line graphed at the right.

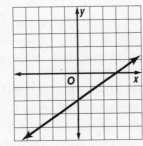

10. _____

11. Graph the line with y-intercept 3 and slope $-\frac{3}{4}$.

11.

Assessment

12. Write an equation in slope-intercept form for the line that passes through $(-1, -2)$ and $(3, 4)$.

12. _____

13. Write an equation in standard form for the line whose slope is undefined and passes through $(-6, 4)$.

13. _____

14. Write an equation in point-slope form for the line that has slope $\frac{1}{3}$ and passes through $(-2, 8)$.

14. _____

15. Write the standard form of the equation $y + 4 = -\frac{12}{7}(x - 1)$.

15. _____

16. Write the slope-intercept form of the equation $y - 2 = 3(x - 4)$.

16. _____

17. Write the slope-intercept form of the equation of the line parallel to the graph of $2x + y = 5$ that passes through $(0, 1)$.

17. _____

18. Write the slope-intercept form of the equation of the line perpendicular to the graph of $y = -\frac{3}{2}x - 7$ that passes through $(3, -2)$.

18. _____

For Questions 19 and 20, use the data in the table.

Time Spent Studying (min)	10	20	30	40	50
Score Received (percent)	53	67	78	87	95

19. Make a scatter plot relating time spent studying to the score received.

19.

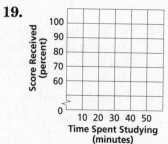

20. Write the slope-intercept form of the equation for a line of fit for the data. Use your equation to predict a student's score if the student spent 35 minutes studying.

20. _____

Bonus In a certain lake, a 1-year-old bluegill fish is 3 inches long, while a 4-year-old bluegill fish is 6.6 inches long. Assuming the growth rate can be approximated by a linear equation, write an equation in slope-intercept form for the length ℓ of a bluegill fish in inches after t years. Then use the equation to determine the age of a 9-inch bluegill.

B: _____

5 **Chapter 5 Test, Form 2D**   SCORE _____

For Questions 1–3, find the slope of the line passing through each pair of points. If the slope is undefined, write "undefined."

1. (4, 1) and (−4, 1)   1. _____

2. (−2, 1) and (3, −2)   2. _____

3. (−6, 7) and (−6, −2)   3. _____

4. Find the value of r so that the line through (4, 5) and   4. _____

   $(r, 3)$ has a slope of $\frac{2}{3}$.

5. In 1983, 57.5% of college students graduated in 5 or fewer   5. _____
   years of study. In 1997, that number had fallen to 52.8%.
   What was the change of rate for percent of students
   graduating within 5 years from 1983 to 1997?

6. Graph $y = \frac{2}{3}x$.   6.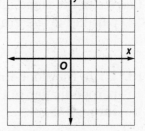

7. If a snail travels 200 inches in 2 hours, how long will it take   7. _____
   the snail to travel 50 inches?

8. Write a linear equation in slope-intercept form to model   8. _____
   the situation: An Internet company charges $4.95 per
   month plus $2.50 for each hour of use.

9. Write an equation in standard form of the line that passes   9. _____
   through (3, 1) and has a y-intercept of −2.

10. Write the slope-intercept form   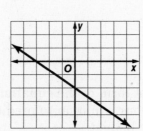   10. _____
    of an equation for the
    line graphed at the right.

11. Graph the line with y-intercept 2   11.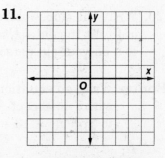
    and slope $-\frac{1}{2}$.

5 **Chapter 5 Test, Form 2D** *(continued)*

12. Write an equation in slope-intercept form for the line that passes through $(5, 4)$ and $(6, -1)$.

12. _____

13. Write an equation in standard form for the line whose slope is undefined that passes through $(5, -3)$.

13. _____

14. Write an equation in point-slope form for the line that has slope $\frac{4}{3}$ and passes through $(3, 0)$.

14. _____

15. Write the standard form of the equation $y - 3 = -\frac{2}{3}(x + 5)$.

15. _____

16. Write the slope-intercept form of the equation $y - 1 = \frac{3}{4}(x - 3)$.

16. _____

17. Write the slope-intercept form of the equation of the line parallel to the graph of $9x + 3y = 6$ that passes through $(5, 3)$.

17. _____

18. Write the slope-intercept form of the equation of the line perpendicular to the graph of $4x - y = 12$ that passes through $(8, 2)$.

18. _____

For Questions 19 and 20, use the data that shows age and percent of budget spent on entertainment in the table.

Age	30	40	50	60	70	80
Percent Spent on Entertainment	6.1	6.0	5.4	5.0	4.7	3.4

19. Make a scatter plot relating the age to the percent of the person's budget spent on entertainment.

19.

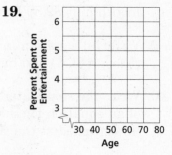

20. Write the slope-intercept form of the equation for a line of fit for the data. Use your equation to predict the percent of a 65-year-old person's budget.

20. _____

Bonus Write an equation in slope-intercept form of the line with y-intercept -6 and parallel to a line perpendicular to $5x + 6y - 13 = 0$.

B: _____

5 Chapter 5 Test, Form 3

SCORE _____

For Questions 1 and 2, find the slope of the line passing through each pair of points. If the slope is undefined, write "undefined."

1. $(-8, 7)$ and $(5, -2)$

1. _____

2. $(5, 9)$ and $(5, -3)$

2. _____

3. Find the value of r so that the line through $(-4, 3)$ and $(r, -3)$ has a slope of $\frac{2}{3}$.

3. _____

4. Find the value of r so that the line through $(r, 5)$ and $(6, r)$ has a slope of $\frac{5}{8}$.

4. _____

5. In 1990, there were approximately 35,000 people in Lancaster. Five years later, the population was 38,452. Find the rate of change in the population.

5. _____

6. Graph $y = -\frac{3}{4}x$.

6.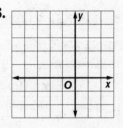

7. If an ostrich can run 15 kilometers in 15 minutes, how many kilometers can it run in an hour?

7. _____

8. Write the point-slope form of an equation of the line that has slope $-\frac{3}{5}$ and passes through $(2, 1)$.

8. _____

9. Write an equation in standard form of the line that passes through $(2, -3)$ and $(-3, 7)$.

9. _____

10. Graph a line whose x-intercept is 5 and whose slope is $-\frac{3}{5}$.

10.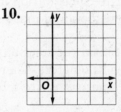

11. Write $y + 4 = -\frac{2}{3}(x - 9)$ in standard form.

11. _____

12. Write the point-slope form of the equation for the line that has x-intercept -3 and y-intercept -2.

12. _____

Assessment

5 **Chapter 5 Test, Form 3** *(continued)*

For Questions 13–20, write an equation in slope-intercept form of the line satisfying the given conditions.

13. has y-intercept -8 and slope 3

13. _____

14. has slope $\frac{5}{2}$ and passes through $(4, -1)$

14. _____

15. passes through $(-3, 7)$ and $(2, 4)$

15. _____

16. is horizontal and passes through $(-4, 6)$

16. _____

17. is parallel to the y-axis and has an x-intercept of 3

17. _____

18. is perpendicular to $4y = 3x - 8$ and passes through $(-12, 7)$

18. _____

19. is parallel to $3x - 5y = 7$ and passes through $(0, -6)$

19. _____

20. is perpendicular to the y-axis and passes through $(-2, 5)$

20. _____

For Questions 21–23, use the data in the table.

21. Make a scatter plot relating the verbal scores and the math scores.

21.

State Graduation Scores

Year	Verbal Score	Math Score
1970	460	488
1980	424	466
1990	410	463
2000	420	460

(Math Score axis: 500, 490, 480, 470, 460, 450; Verbal Score axis: 400 420 440 460 480)

22. Does the scatter plot in Question 21 show a *positive*, a *negative*, or *no correlation*? What does that relationship represent?

22. _____

23. Write the equation for a line of fit. Predict the corresponding math score for a verbal score of 445.

23. _____

24. A rental car company charges $52.99 per day, including 200 free kilometers. There is a charge of $0.12/km for additional kilometers. Write a linear equation that models this situation.

24. _____

25. Write the slope-intercept form of $y + 3 = -0.5(x - 10)$.

25. _____

Bonus The area of a circle varies directly as the square of the radius. If the radius is tripled, by what factor will the area increase?

B: _____

5 **Chapter 5 Open-Ended Assessment**   SCORE _____

Demonstrate your knowledge by giving a clear, concise solution to each problem. Be sure to include all relevant drawings and justify your answers. You may show your solution in more than one way or investigate beyond the requirements of the problem.

1. Draw a line on a coordinate plane so that you can determine at least two points on the graph.

   a. Describe how you would determine the slope of the graph and justify the slope you found.

   b. Explain how you could use the slope to write various forms of the equation of that line. Then write three forms of the equation.

2. You are told that a line passes through $(-2, 3)$.

   a. Discuss what other information you would need to graph this line.

   b. Then describe how you would use that information to graph the line and write its equation.

3. Refer to the scatter plot at the right.

   a. Describe the pattern of points in the scatter plot and the relationship between x and y.

   b. Give at least two examples of real-life situations that, if graphed, would result in a correlation like the one shown in this scatter plot.

   c. Add a scale and heading to each axis. Then write an equation that would model the points represented by this plot.

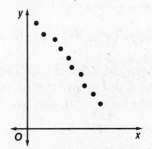

4. The table gives the life expectancy of a child born in the United States in a given year.

   a. Make a scatter plot of the data.

   b. Can you use the data to claim that the increase in life expectancy is due to improved health care? Explain your response.

   c. Use the data to predict the life expectancy of a baby born in 2000. Explain how you determined your answer.

Years of Life Expected at Birth	
Year of Birth	Life Expectancy (years)
1920	54.1
1930	59.7
1940	62.9
1950	68.2
1960	69.7
1970	70.8
1980	73.7
1985	74.7
1990	75.4
1995	75.8

Source: National Center for Health Statistics

Assessment

5 Chapter 5 Vocabulary Test/Review

SCORE _____

best-fit line	linear interpolation	point-slope form	slope
constant of variation	line of fit	positive correlation	slope-intercept form
direct variation	negative correlation	rate of change	standard form
family of graphs	parallel lines	scatter plot	
linear extrapolation	perpendicular lines		

Choose from the terms above to complete each sentence.

1. If two lines have slopes that are negative reciprocals of each other, then they are _____. If they have slopes that are the same, then they are _____.

2. In the equation, $y = kx$, k represents the _____.

3. A graph of data points is sometimes called a _____.

4. Several graphs who have one or more common characteristics form a

   _____.

5. Earning $7.50 per hour is an example of a _____.

6. The leftmost data point in a set is (3, 27) and the rightmost point is (12, 13). If you use a linear prediction equation to find the corresponding y value for $x = 10$, you are using a method called

   _____.

7. The ratio of the rise to the run or the ratio of the change in the y-coordinates to the change in the x-coordinates are definitions of

   _____.

8. The equation $y = -3x + 12$ is written in _____ form.

9. The equation $y + 6 = 2(x - 4)$ is written in _____ form.

10. The equation $3x + y = 12$ is written in _____ form.

In your own words—
Define each term.

11. line of fit

12. linear extrapolation

5 # Chapter 5 Quiz
(Lessons 5–1 and 5–2)

Determine the slope of the line passing through each pair of points.

1. $(5, 8)$ and $(-4, 6)$

2. $(9, 4)$ and $(5, -3)$

3. $(-3, 10)$ and $(-3, 6)$

4. In 1996, there were approximately 275 students in the Delaware High School band. In 2002, that number increased to 305. Find the annual rate of change in the number of students in the band.

5. Chris's wages vary directly as the time she works. If her wages for 20 hours are $150, what are her wages for 38 hours?

1. _____

2. _____

3. _____

4. _____

5. _____

----

5 # Chapter 5 Quiz
(Lessons 5–3 and 5–4)

Write the slope-intercept form of the equation for each situation.

1. slope: $\frac{1}{4}$, y-intercept: -5

2. line passing through $(9, 2)$ and $(-2, 6)$

3. Graph $4x + 3y = 12$.

1. _____

2. _____

3.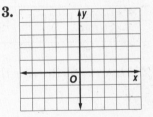

4. Write a linear equation in slope-intercept form to model a tree 4 feet tall that grows 3 inches per year.

4. _____

5. **STANDARDIZED TEST PRACTICE** The table of ordered pairs shows the coordinates of the two points on the graph of a function. Which equation describes the function?

x	y
-2	2
4	-1

A. $y = -2x + 1$ **B.** $y = \frac{1}{2}x - 1$

C. $y = -\frac{1}{2}x + 1$ **D.** $y = -\frac{1}{2}x - 1$

5. _____

Assessment

5 Chapter 5 Quiz

(Lessons 5–5 and 5–6)

1. Write the point-slope form of an equation for a line passing through (3, 6) with slope $m = -\frac{1}{3}$.

   1. _____

2. Write $y - 9 = -(x + 2)$ in slope-intercept form.

   2. _____

3. Write the point-slope form of an equation for the horizontal line that passes through $(-4, -1)$.

   3. _____

4. Write the slope-intercept form of an equation for the line that passes through (5, 3) and is parallel to $x + 3y = 6$.

   4. _____

5. Write the slope-intercept form of an equation for the line that passes through (0, 3) and is perpendicular to $9x - 4y = -8$.

   5. _____

---

5 Chapter 5 Quiz

(Lesson 5–7)

1. Use the data in the table to make a scatter plot relating age to median income.

Age	26	27	28	29	30
Median Income ($1000)	16.8	19.1	23.3	25.8	33.9

   1–2.

2. Draw a fit line for the scatter plot.

3. Do the data show a positive or negative relationship? What does this relationship mean?

   3. _____

4. Write the slope-intercept form of an equation for a line of fit.

   4. _____

5. Use the line of fit to predict the median income for someone 32 years old.

   5. _____

5 # Chapter 5 Mid-Chapter Test

SCORE _____

(Lessons 5–1 through 5–4)

Part I *Write the letter for the correct answer in the blank at the right of each question.*

1. Find the slope of the line through $(6, -7)$ and $(4, -8)$.

    A. $-\dfrac{1}{2}$ **B.** 2   **C.** $\dfrac{1}{2}$ **D.** -2 1. _____

2. Find the slope of the line through $(0, 5)$ and $(5, 5)$.

    A. 0   **B.** 1   **C.** 2   **D.** no slope   2. _____

3. In 1999, 96.60 quadrillion Btu (British thermal units) of energy were consumed in the United States. In 1995, 90.86 quadrillion Btu were consumed. Which of the following is the rate of change in consumption from 1995 to 1999?

    A. 1.44 quadrillion btu per year

    B. 5.74 quadrillion btu per year

    C. 0.69 years per quadrillion btu

    D. 0.57 quadrillion btu per year   3. _____

4. The total price of a bag of peaches varies directly with the cost per pound. If 3 pounds of peaches cost $3.60, how much would 5.5 pounds cost?

    A. $1.20   **B.** $6.60   **C.** $6.00   **D.** $1.96   4. _____

5. Which is the slope-intercept form of an equation for the line containing $(0, -3)$ with slope -1?

    A. $y = -x - 3$ **B.** $y = -3x - 1$ **C.** $y = x + 3$ **D.** $x = -3y - 1$ 5. _____

Part II

For Questions 6–8, write an equation in slope-intercept form of the line satisfying the given conditions.

6. has y-intercept 5 and slope $-\dfrac{3}{4}$ 6. _____

7. passes through $(4, 2)$ and $(0, -2)$ 7. _____

8. has slope -3 and passes through $(2, -4)$ 8. _____

For Questions 9 and 10, use the graph at the right.

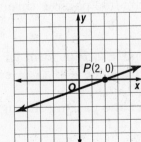

9. What is the slope of the line shown in the graph?   9. _____

10. What is the equation of the line shown in the graph?   10. _____

Assessment

Glencoe Algebra 1

5 Chapter 5 Cumulative Review
(Chapters 1–5)

1. Write $2 \cdot r \cdot r \cdot s \cdot s$ using exponents. (Lesson 1-1)

1. _____

2. Evaluate $2xy - y^2$ if $x = 6$ and $y = 12$. (Lesson 1-2)

2. _____

Simplify each expression. (Lessons 2-3 through 2-5)

3. _____

3. $4\frac{7}{8} - 2\frac{5}{8}$ 4. $\frac{3}{8} \cdot 2\frac{7}{18}$

4. _____

5. _____

5. $-\frac{2}{3} + \frac{3}{4}$ 6. $-3.9 + (-2.5) + (-8.7)$

6. _____

7. _____

7. $4(2y + y) - 6(4y + 3y)$ 8. $\frac{12a - 18b}{-6}$

8. _____

For Questions 9–11, solve each equation. (Lessons 3-2 through 3-4)

9. $13 - m = 21$

9. _____

10. $\frac{3}{4}x = \frac{2}{3}$

10. _____

11. $4x + 12 = -16$

11. _____

12. Solve $x - 2y = 12$ if the domain is $\{-3, -1, 0, 2, 5\}$. (Lesson 4-4)

12. _____

13. Determine whether $\{(1, 4), (2, 6), (3, 7), (4, 4)\}$ is a function, and explain your reasoning. (Lesson 4-6)

13. _____

14. Write an equation for the relationship between the variables in the chart. (Lesson 4-8)

14. _____

x	0	2	4	6
y	2	5	8	11

15. Determine the slope of the line passing through $(2, 7)$ and $(-5, 2)$. (Lesson 5-1)

15. _____

16. Write an equation in slope-intercept form for the line passing through $(2, 6)$ with slope -3. (Lesson 5-3)

16. _____

17. Write an equation for the line passing through $(-6, 5)$ and $(-6, -4)$. (Lesson 5-4)

17. _____

18. Write the slope-intercept form of an equation for the line that is parallel to $5x - 3y = 1$ and passes through $(0, -4)$. (Lesson 5-6)

18. _____

5 Standardized Test Practice
(Chapters 1–5)

Part 1: Multiple Choice

Instructions: Fill in the appropriate oval for the best answer.

1. If $a = 2$, $b = 6$, and $c = 4$, then $\dfrac{(4a - b)^2}{b + c} = ?$ (Lesson 1-2)

   A. 4   **B.** 0.4   **C.** 40   **D.** 0.04

   1. Ⓐ Ⓑ Ⓒ Ⓓ

2. If $4 + 7 + 6 = 4 + 7 + 6 + n$, what is the value of n? (Lesson 1-4)

   E. 0   **F.** 1   **G.** 4   **H.** 6

   2. Ⓔ Ⓕ Ⓖ Ⓗ

3. Lynn has 4 more books than José. If Lynn gives José 6 of her books, how many more will José have than Lynn? (Lesson 2-3)

   A. 2   **B.** 4   **C.** 8   **D.** 10

   3. Ⓐ Ⓑ Ⓒ Ⓓ

4. If $x = \dfrac{16}{24}$, which value of x does NOT form a proportion? (Lesson 2-6)

   E. $\dfrac{2}{3}$ **F.** $\dfrac{3}{4}$ **G.** $\dfrac{12}{18}$ **H.** $\dfrac{32}{48}$

   4. Ⓔ Ⓕ Ⓖ Ⓗ

5. Two-thirds of a number added to itself is 20. What is the number? (Lesson 3-1)

   A. 12   **B.** 13   **C.** 30   **D.** 33

   5. Ⓐ Ⓑ Ⓒ Ⓓ

6. 16% of 980 is 9.8% of what number? (Lesson 3-5)

   E. 1.6   **F.** 16   **G.** 160   **H.** 1600

   6. Ⓔ Ⓕ Ⓖ Ⓗ

7. For what value(s) of r is $3r - 6 = 7 + 3r$? (Lesson 3-7)

   A. all numbers   **B.** all negative integers
   C. 0   **D.** no values of r

   7. Ⓐ Ⓑ Ⓒ Ⓓ

8. The range of a relation includes the integers $\dfrac{x}{4}$, $\dfrac{x}{5}$, and $\dfrac{x}{8}$. What could be a value for x in the domain? (Lesson 4-3)

   E. 20   **F.** 30   **G.** 32   **H.** 40

   8. Ⓔ Ⓕ Ⓖ Ⓗ

9. A line with a slope of -1 passes through points at $(2, 3)$ and $(5, y)$. Find the value of y. (Lesson 5-1)

   A. -6 **B.** -3 **C.** 0   **D.** 6

   9. Ⓐ Ⓑ Ⓒ Ⓓ

10. If a line passes through $(0, -6)$ and has a slope of -3, what is an equation for the line? (Lesson 5-4)

    E. $y = -6x - 3$ **F.** $x = -6y - 3$
    G. $y = -3x - 6$ **H.** $x = -3y - 6$

    10. Ⓔ Ⓕ Ⓖ Ⓗ

Assessment

5 # Standardized Test Practice *(continued)*

Part 2: Grid In

Instructions: Enter your answer by writing each digit of the answer in a column box and then shading in the appropriate oval that corresponds to that entry.

11. If $x^2 = 16$ and $y^2 = 4$, what is the greatest possible value of $(x - y)^2$? (Lesson 2-8)

12. If $\dfrac{x + 2x + 3x}{2} = 6$, $x = ?$ (Lesson 3-4)

11.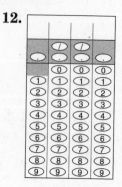

12.

13. The formula for the volume of a rectangular solid is $V = Bh$. A packing crate has a height of 4.5 inches and a base area of 18.2 square inches. What is the volume of the crate in cubic inches? (Lesson 3-8)

14. Find the slope of a line parallel to $2y = x + 6$. (Lesson 5-6)

13.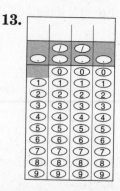

14.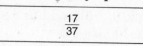

Part 3: Quantitative Comparison

Instructions: Compare the quantities in columns A and B. Shade in
- (A) if the quantity in column A is greater;
- (B) if the quantity in column B is greater;
- (C) if the quantities are equal; or
- (D) if the relationship cannot be determined from the information given.

Column A   **Column B**

15.

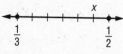

On the number line above, the marks are equally spaced.

x

$\dfrac{17}{37}$

15. (A) (B) (C) (D)

(Lesson 2-1)

16. $3x + 5 = 20$

$6x$

40

16. (A) (B) (C) (D)

(Lesson 3-4)

5 Standardized Test Practice

Student Record Sheet *(Use with pages 314–315 of the Student Edition.)*

Select the best answer from the choices given and fill in the corresponding oval.

1 Ⓐ Ⓑ Ⓒ Ⓓ   4 Ⓐ Ⓑ Ⓒ Ⓓ   7 Ⓐ Ⓑ Ⓒ Ⓓ

2 Ⓐ Ⓑ Ⓒ Ⓓ   5 Ⓐ Ⓑ Ⓒ Ⓓ   8 Ⓐ Ⓑ Ⓒ Ⓓ

3 Ⓐ Ⓑ Ⓒ Ⓓ   6 Ⓐ Ⓑ Ⓒ Ⓓ   9 Ⓐ Ⓑ Ⓒ Ⓓ

Solve the problem and write your answer in the blank.

For Questions 10, 12, and 14, also enter your answer by writing each number or symbol in a box. Then fill in the corresponding oval for that number or symbol.

10 _____ (grid in)

11 _____

12 _____ (grid in)

13 _____

14 _____ (grid in)

15 _____

16 _____

17 _____

10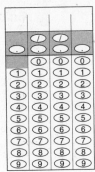

12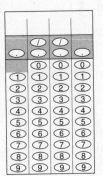

14

Answers

Record your answers for Questions 18–19 on the back of this paper.

Answers (Lesson 5-1)

5-1 Study Guide and Intervention

Slope

Find Slope

Slope of a Line	$m = \dfrac{\text{rise}}{\text{run}}$ or $m = \dfrac{y_2 - y_1}{x_2 - x_1}$, where (x_1, y_1) and (x_2, y_2) are the coordinates of any two points on a nonvertical line

Example 1 Find the slope of the line that passes through $(-3, 5)$ and $(4, -2)$.

Let $(-3, 5) = (x_1, y_1)$ and $(4, -2) = (x_2, y_2)$.

$m = \dfrac{y_2 - y_1}{x_2 - x_1}$ Slope formula

$= \dfrac{-2 - 5}{4 - (-3)}$

$= \dfrac{-7}{7}$

$= -1$ Simplify.

Example 2 Find the value of r so that the line through $(10, r)$ and $(3, 4)$ has a slope of $-\dfrac{2}{7}$.

$m = \dfrac{y_2 - y_1}{x_2 - x_1}$ Slope formula

$-\dfrac{2}{7} = \dfrac{4 - r}{3 - 10}$ $m = -\dfrac{2}{7}, y_2 = 4, y_1 = r, x_2 = 3, x_1 = 10$

$-\dfrac{2}{7} = \dfrac{4 - r}{-7}$ Simplify.

$-2(-7) = 7(4 - r)$ Cross multiply.

$14 = 28 - 7r$ Distributive Property

$-14 = -7r$ Subtract 28 from each side.

$2 = r$ Divide each side by -7.

Exercises

Find the slope of the line that passes through each pair of points.

1. $(4, 9), (1, 6)$ **1**

2. $(-4, -1), (-2, -5)$ **−2**

3. $(-4, -1), (-4, -5)$ **undefined**

4. $(2, 1), (8, 9)$ $\dfrac{4}{3}$

5. $(14, -8), (7, -6)$ $-\dfrac{2}{7}$

6. $(4, -3), (8, -3)$ **0**

7. $(1, -2), (6, 2)$ $\dfrac{4}{5}$

8. $(2, 5), (6, 2)$ $-\dfrac{3}{4}$

9. $(4, 3.5), (-4, 3.5)$ **0**

Determine the value of r so the line that passes through each pair of points has the given slope.

10. $(6, 8), (r, -2), m = 1$ **−4**

11. $(-1, -3), (7, r), m = \dfrac{3}{4}$ **3**

12. $(2, 8), (r, -4) \; m = -3$ **6**

13. $(7, -5), (6, r), m = 0$ **−5**

14. $(r, 4), (7, 1), m = \dfrac{3}{4}$ **−3**

15. $(7, 5), (r, 9), m = 6$ $\dfrac{23}{3}$

16. $(10, r), (3, 4), m = -\dfrac{2}{7}$ **2**

17. $(10, 4), (-2, r), m = -0.5$ **10**

18. $(r, 3), (7, r), m = -\dfrac{1}{5}$ **2**

Lesson 5-1

5-1 Study Guide and Intervention (continued)

Slope

Rate of Change The rate of change tells, on average, how a quantity is changing over time. Slope describes a rate of change.

Example POPULATION The graph shows the population growth in China.

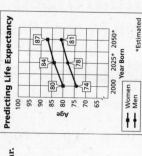

Population Growth in China

Source: United Nations Population Division

a. Find the rates of change for 1950–1975 and for 1975–2000.

1950–1975: $\dfrac{\text{change in population}}{\text{change in time}} = \dfrac{0.93 - 0.55}{1975 - 1950}$

$= \dfrac{0.38}{25}$ or 0.0152

1975–2000: $\dfrac{\text{change in population}}{\text{change in time}} = \dfrac{1.24 - 0.93}{2000 - 1975}$

$= \dfrac{0.31}{25}$ or 0.0124

b. Explain the meaning of the slope in each case.

From 1950–1975, the growth was 0.0152 billion per year, or 15.2 million per year. From 1975–2000, the growth was 0.0124 billion per year, or 12.4 million per year.

c. How are the different rates of change shown on the graph?

There is a greater vertical change for 1950–1975 than for 1975–2000. Therefore, the section of the graph for 1950–1975 has a steeper slope.

Exercises

LONGEVITY The graph shows the predicted life expectancy for men and women born in a given year.

Predicting Life Expectancy

Source: USA TODAY

1. Find the rates of change for women from 2000–2025 and 2025–2050. **0.16/yr, 0.12/yr**

2. Find the rates of change for men from 2000–2025 and 2025–2050. **0.16/yr, 0.12/yr**

3. Explain the meaning of your results in Exercises 1 and 2. **Both men and women increased their life expectancy at the same rates.**

4. What pattern do you see in the increase with each 25-year period? **While life expectancy increases, it does not increase at a constant rate.**

5. Make a prediction for the life expectancy for 2050–2075. Explain how you arrived at your prediction. **Sample answer: 89 for women and 83 for men; the decrease in rate from 2000–2025 to 2025–2050 is 0.04/yr. If the decrease in the rate remains the same, the change of rate for 2050–2075 might be 0.08/yr and 25(0.08) = 2 years of increase over the 25-year span.**

Practice (Average)

5-1

Slope

Find the slope of the line that passes through each pair of points.

1.  −3

2. $\frac{4}{5}$

3. 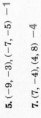 0

4. (6, 3), (7, −4) −7

5. (−9, −3), (−7, −5) −1

6. (6, −2), (5, −4) 2

7. (7, −4), (4, 8) −4

8. (−7, 8), (−7, 5) undefined

9. (5, 9), (3, 9) 0

10. (15, 2), (−6, 5) $-\frac{1}{7}$

11. (3, 9), (−2, 8) $\frac{1}{5}$

12. (−2, −5), (7, 8) $\frac{13}{9}$

13. (12, 10), (12, 5) undefined

14. (0.2, −0.9), (0.5, −0.9) 0

15. $\left(\frac{7}{3}, \frac{4}{3}\right)$, $\left(-\frac{1}{3}, \frac{2}{3}\right)$ $\frac{1}{4}$

Find the value of *r* so the line that passes through each pair of points has the given slope.

16. (−2, r), (6, 7), $m = \frac{1}{2}$ 3

17. (−4, 3), (r, 5), $m = \frac{1}{4}$ 4

18. (−3, −4), (−5, r), $m = -\frac{9}{2}$ 5

19. (−5, r), (1, 3), $m = \frac{7}{6}$ −4

20. (1, 4), (r, 5), m undefined 1

21. (−7, 2), (−8, r), m = −5 7

22. (r, 7), (11, 8), $m = -\frac{1}{5}$ 16

23. (r, 2), (5, r), m = 0 2

24. **ROOFING** The *pitch* of a roof is the number of feet the roof rises for each 12 feet horizontally. If a roof has a pitch of 8, what is its slope expressed as a positive number? $\frac{2}{3}$

25. **SALES** A daily newspaper had 12,125 subscribers when it began publication. Five years later it had 10,100 subscribers. What is the average yearly rate of change in the number of subscribers for the five-year period? −405 subscribers per year

© Glencoe/McGraw-Hill

284

Glencoe Algebra 1

Skills Practice

5-1

Slope

Find the slope of the line that passes through each pair of points.

1. 2

2.  $\frac{1}{3}$

3.  −3

4. (2, 5), (3, 6) 1

5. (6, 1), (−6, 1) 0

6. (4, 6), (4, 8) undefined

7. (5, 2), (5, −2) undefined

8. (2, 5), (−3, −5) 2

9. (9, 8), (7, −8) 8

10. (−5, −8), (−8, 1) −3

11. (−3, 10), (−3, 7) undefined

12. (17, 18), (18, 17) −1

13. (−6, −4), (4, 1) $\frac{1}{2}$

14. (10, 0), (−2, 4) $-\frac{1}{3}$

15. (2, −1), (−8, −2) $\frac{1}{10}$

16. (5, −9), (3, −2) $-\frac{7}{2}$

17. (12, 6), (3, −5) $\frac{11}{9}$

18. (−4, 5), (−8, −5) $\frac{5}{2}$

19. (−5, 6), (7, −8) $-\frac{7}{6}$

Find the value of *r* so the line that passes through each pair of points has the given slope.

20. (r, 3), (5, 9), m = 2 2

21. (5, 9), (r, −3), m = −4 8

22. (r, 2), (6, 3), $m = \frac{1}{2}$ 4

23. (r, 4), (7, 1), $m = \frac{3}{4}$ 11

24. (5, 3), (r, −5), m = 4 3

25. (7, r), (4, 6), m = 0 6

© Glencoe/McGraw-Hill

283

Glencoe Algebra 1

Lesson 5-1

Answers

Left page: Reading to Learn Mathematics

5-1 Reading to Learn Mathematics

Slope

Pre-Activity **Why is slope important in architecture?**

Read the introduction to Lesson 5-1 at the top of page 256 in your textbook. Then complete the definition of slope and fill in the boxes on the graph with the words *rise* and *run*.

$$\text{slope} = \frac{\text{rise}}{\text{run}}$$

In this graph, the rise is __3__ units, and the run is __5__ units.

Thus, the slope of this line is $\frac{3 \text{ units}}{5 \text{ units}}$ or $\frac{3}{5}$.

Reading the Lesson

1. Describe each type of slope and include a sketch.

Type of Slope	Description of Graph	Sketch
positive	The graph rises as you go from left to right.	
negative	The graph falls as you go from left to right.	
zero	The graph is a horizontal line.	
undefined	The graph is a vertical line.	

2. Describe how each expression is related to *slope*.

a. $\frac{y_2 - y_1}{x_2 - x_1}$ difference of *y*-coordinates divided by difference of corresponding *x*-coordinates

b. $\frac{\text{rise}}{\text{run}}$ how far up or down as compared to how far left or right

c. $52,000 increase in spending   slope used as rate of change
26 months

Helping You Remember

3. The word *rise* is usually associated with going up. Sometimes going from one point on the graph does not involve a rise and a run but a fall and a run. Describe how you could select points so that it is always a rise from the first point to the second point. **Sample answer: If the slope is negative, choose the second point so that its *x*-coordinate is less than that of the first point.**

Right page: Enrichment

5-1 Enrichment

Treasure Hunt with Slopes

Using the definition of slope, draw lines with the slopes listed below. A correct solution will trace the route to the treasure.

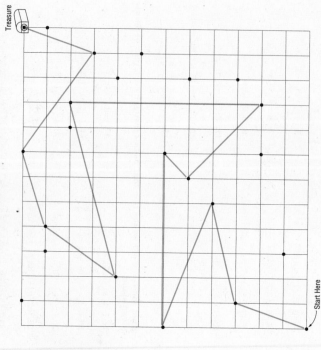

1. 3
2. $\frac{1}{4}$
3. $-\frac{2}{5}$
4. 0

5. 1
6. -1
7. no slope
8. $\frac{2}{7}$

9. $\frac{3}{2}$
10. $\frac{1}{3}$
11. $-\frac{3}{4}$
12. 3

Lesson 5-1

Page 287 (left)

NAME _____ DATE _____ PERIOD _____

5-2 Study Guide and Intervention
Slope and Direct Variation

Direct Variation A direct variation is described by an equation of the form $y = kx$, where $k \neq 0$. We say that y varies directly as x. In the equation $y = kx$, k is the **constant of variation**.

Example 1 Name the constant of variation for the equation. Then find the slope of the line that passes through the pair of points.

For $y = \frac{1}{2}x$, the constant of variation is $\frac{1}{2}$.

$$m = \frac{y_2 - y_1}{x_2 - x_1} \quad \text{Slope formula}$$

$$= \frac{1 - 0}{2 - 0} \quad (x_1, y_1) = (0, 0), (x_2, y_2) = (2, 1)$$

$$= \frac{1}{2} \quad \text{Simplify.}$$

The slope is $\frac{1}{2}$.

Example 2 Suppose y varies directly as x, and $y = 30$ when $x = 5$.

a. Write a direct variation equation that relates x and y.

Find the value of k.

$y = kx$ Direct variation equation
$30 = k(5)$ Replace y with 30 and x with 5.
$6 = k$ Divide each side by 5.

Therefore, the equation is $y = 6x$.

b. Use the direct variation equation to find x when $y = 18$.

$y = 6x$ Direct variation equation
$18 = 6x$ Replace y with 18.
$3 = x$ Divide each side by 6.

Therefore, $x = 3$ when $y = 18$.

Exercises

Name the constant of variation for each equation. Then determine the slope of the line that passes through each pair of points.

1.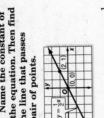

$-2; -2$

2.

$3; 3$

3.

$\frac{3}{2}; \frac{3}{2}$

Write a direct variation equation that relates x to y. Assume that y varies directly as x. Then solve.

4. If $y = 4$ when $x = 2$, find y when $x = 16$. $y = 2x; 32$

5. If $y = 9$ when $x = -3$, find x when $y = 6$. $y = -3x; -2$

6. If $y = -4.8$ when $x = -1.6$, find x when $y = -24$. $y = 3x; -8$

7. If $y = \frac{1}{4}$ when $x = \frac{1}{8}$, find x when $y = \frac{3}{16}$. $y = 2x; \frac{3}{32}$

© Glencoe/McGraw-Hill   287   Glencoe Algebra 1

Page 288 (right)

NAME _____ DATE _____ PERIOD _____

5-2 Study Guide and Intervention (continued)
Slope and Direct Variation

Solve Problems The distance formula $d = rt$ is a direct variation equation. In the formula, distance d varies directly as time t, and the rate r is the constant of variation.

Example TRAVEL A family drove their car 225 miles in 5 hours.

a. Write a direct variation equation to find the distance traveled for any number of hours.

Use given values for d and t to find r.

$d = rt$ Original equation
$225 = r(5)$ $d = 225$ and $t = 5$
$45 = r$ Divide each side by 5.

Therefore, the direct variation equation is $d = 45t$.

b. Graph the equation.

The graph of $d = 45t$ passes through the origin with slope 45.

$$m = \frac{45}{1} \quad \frac{\text{rise}}{\text{run}}$$

✓**CHECK** (5, 225) lies on the graph.

Automobile Trips

c. Estimate how many hours it would take the family to drive 360 miles.

$d = 45t$ Original equation
$360 = 45t$ Replace d with 360.
$t = 8$ Divide each side by 45.

Therefore, it will take 8 hours to drive 360 miles.

Exercises

RETAIL The total cost C of bulk jelly beans is $4.49 times the number of pounds p.

1. Write a direct variation equation that relates the variables. $C = 4.49p$

2. Graph the equation on the grid at the right.

3. Find the cost of $\frac{3}{4}$ pound of jelly beans. $3.37

Cost of Jelly Beans

CHEMISTRY Charles's Law states that, at a constant pressure, volume of a gas V varies directly as its temperature T. A volume of 4 cubic feet of a certain gas has a temperature of 200° (absolute temperature).

4. Write a direct variation equation that relates the variables. $V = 0.02T$

5. Graph the equation on the grid at the right.

6. Find the volume of the same gas at 250° (absolute temperature). 5 ft^3

Charles's Law

© Glencoe/McGraw-Hill   288   Glencoe Algebra 1

Answers

Skills Practice (page 289)

NAME _____ DATE _____ PERIOD _____

5-2 Skills Practice
Slope and Direct Variation

Name the constant of variation for each equation. Then determine the slope of the line that passes through each pair of points.

1. $y = \frac{1}{3}x$; $\frac{1}{3}$, $\frac{1}{3}$

2. 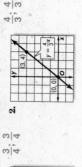 $y = -2x$; -2, -2

3. 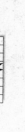 $y = \frac{3}{2}x$; $\frac{3}{2}$, $\frac{3}{2}$

Graph each equation.

4. $y = 3x$

5. $y = -\frac{3}{4}x$

6. $y = \frac{2}{5}x$

Write a direct variation equation that relates x and y. Assume that y varies directly as x. Then solve.

7. If $y = -8$ when $x = -2$, find x when $y = 32$. $y = 4x$; 8

8. If $y = 45$ when $x = 15$, find x when $y = 15$. $y = 3x$; 5

9. If $y = -4$ when $x = 2$, find y when $x = -6$. $y = -2x$; 12

10. If $y = -9$ when $x = 3$, find y when $x = -5$. $y = -3x$; 15

11. If $y = 4$ when $x = 16$, find y when $x = 6$. $y = \frac{1}{4}x$; $\frac{3}{2}$

12. If $y = 12$ when $x = 18$, find y when $y = -16$. $y = \frac{2}{3}x$; -24

Write a direct variation equation that relates the variables. Then graph the equation.

13. **TRAVEL** The total cost C of gasoline is $1.80 times the number of gallons g. $C = 1.80g$

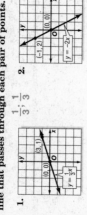

Gasoline Cost

14. **SHIPPING** The number of delivered toys T is 3 times the total number of crates c. $T = 3c$

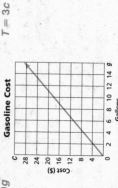

Toys Shipped

Practice (page 290)

NAME _____ DATE _____ PERIOD _____

5-2 Practice (Average)
Slope and Direct Variation

Name the constant of variation for each equation. Then determine the slope of the line that passes through each pair of points.

1. $y = \frac{3}{4}x$; $\frac{3}{4}$, $\frac{3}{4}$

2. 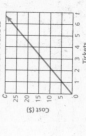 $y = -\frac{4}{3}x$; $\frac{4}{3}$, $\frac{4}{3}$

3. $y = -\frac{5}{2}x$; $-\frac{5}{2}$, $-\frac{5}{2}$

Graph each equation.

4. $y = -2x$

5. $y = \frac{6}{5}x$

6. $y = -\frac{5}{3}x$

Write a direct variation equation that relates x and y. Assume that y varies directly as x. Then solve.

7. If $y = 7.5$ when $x = 0.5$, find y when $x = -0.3$. $y = 15x$; -4.5

8. If $y = 80$ when $x = 32$, find x when $y = 100$. $y = 2.5x$; 40

9. If $y = \frac{3}{4}$ when $x = 24$, find y when $x = 12$. $y = \frac{1}{32}x$; $\frac{3}{8}$

Write a direct variation equation that relates the variables. Then graph the equation.

10. **MEASURE** The width W of a rectangle is two thirds of the length ℓ. $W = \frac{2}{3}\ell$

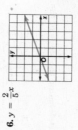

Rectangle Dimensions

11. **TICKETS** The total cost C of tickets is $4.50 times the number of tickets t. $C = 4.50t$

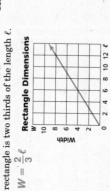

Cost of Tickets

12. **PRODUCE** The cost of bananas varies directly with their weight. Miguel bought $3\frac{1}{2}$ pounds of bananas for $1.12. Write an equation that relates the cost of the bananas to their weight. Then find the cost of $4\frac{1}{4}$ pounds of bananas. $C = 0.32p$; $1.36

NAME _____ DATE _____ PERIOD _____

5-2 Reading to Learn Mathematics

Slope and Direct Variation

Pre-Activity **How is slope related to your shower?**

Read the introduction to Lesson 5-2 at the top of page 264 in your textbook.

- How do the numbers in the table relate to the graph shown?
  They are the coordinates of the points on the graph.

- Think about the first sentence. What does it mean to say that a standard showerhead uses about 6 gallons of water per minute?
  Sample answer: For each minute the shower runs, 6 gallons of water come out. So, if the shower ran 10 minutes, that would be 60 gallons.

Reading the Lesson

1. What is the form of a direct variation equation? $y = kx$

2. How is the constant of variation related to slope? The constant of variation has the same value as the slope of the graph of the equation.

3. The expression "y varies directly as x" can be written as the equation $y = kx$. How would you write an equation for "w varies directly as the square of t"? $w = kt^2$

4. For each situation, write an equation with the proper constant of variation.

   a. The distance d varies directly as time t, and a cheetah can travel 88 feet in 1 second. $d = 88t$

   b. The perimeter p of a pentagon with all sides of equal length varies directly as the length s of a side of the pentagon. A pentagon has 5 sides. $p = 5s$

   c. The wages W earned by an employee vary directly with the number of hours h that are worked. Enrique earned \$172.50 for 23 hours of work. $W = \$7.50h$

Helping You Remember

5. Look up the word *constant* in a dictionary. How does this definition relate to the term constant of variation? **Sample answer: Something unchanging; the constant of variation relates x and y in the same value every time, and that relationship never changes.**

Lesson 5-2

NAME _____ DATE _____ PERIOD _____

5-2 Enrichment

nth Power Variation

An equation of the form $y = kx^n$, where $k \neq 0$, describes an nth power variation. The variable n can be replaced by 2 to indicate the second power of x (the square of x) or by 3 to indicate the third power of x (the cube of x).

Assume that the weight of a person of average build varies directly as the cube of that person's height. The equation of variation has the form $w = kh^3$.

The weight that a person's legs will support is proportional to the cross-sectional area of the leg bones. This area varies directly as the square of the person's height. The equation of variation has the form $s = kh^2$.

Answer each question.

1. For a person 6 feet tall who weighs 200 pounds, find a value for k in the equation $w = kh^3$.
   $k = 0.93$

2. Use your answer from Exercise 1 to predict the weight of a person who is 5 feet tall. about 116 pounds

3. Find the value for k in the equation $w = kh^3$ for a baby who is 20 inches long and weighs 6 pounds.
   $k = 1.296$ for $h = \dfrac{5}{3}$ ft

4. How does your answer to Exercise 3 demonstrate that a baby is significantly fatter in proportion to its height than an adult?
   k has a greater value.

5. For a person 6 feet tall who weighs 200 pounds, find a value for k in the equation $s = kh^2$.
   $k = 5.56$

6. For a baby who is 20 inches long and weighs 6 pounds, find an "infant value" for k in the equation $s = kh^2$.
   $k = 2.16$ for $h = \dfrac{5}{3}$ ft

7. According to the adult equation you found (Exercise 1), how much would an imaginary giant 20 feet tall weigh?
   7440 pounds

8. According to the adult equation for weight supported (Exercise 5), how much weight could a 20-foot tall giant's legs actually support?
   only 2224 pounds

9. What can you conclude from Exercises 7 and 8?
   Answers will vary. For example, bone strength limits the size humans can attain.

Answers

NAME _____ DATE _____ PERIOD _____

5-3 Study Guide and Intervention

Slope-Intercept Form

Slope-Intercept Form | $y = mx + b$, where m is the given slope and b is the y-intercept

Example 1 Write an equation of the line whose slope is -4 and whose y-intercept is 3.

$y = mx + b$ Slope-intercept form
$y = -4x + 3$ Replace m with -4 and b with 3.

Example 2 Graph $3x - 4y = 8$.

$3x - 4y = 8$ Original equation
$-4y = -3x + 8$ Subtract 3x from each side.
$\dfrac{-4y}{-4} = \dfrac{-3x + 8}{-4}$ Divide each side by -4.
$y = \dfrac{3}{4}x - 2$ Simplify.

The y-intercept of $y = \dfrac{3}{4}x - 2$ is -2 and the slope is $\dfrac{3}{4}$. So graph the point $(0, -2)$. From this point, move up 3 units and right 4 units. Draw a line passing through both points.

Exercises

Write an equation of the line with the given slope and y-intercept.

1. slope: 8, y-intercept -3
$y = 8x - 3$

2. slope: -2, y-intercept -1
$y = -2x - 1$

3. slope: -1, y-intercept -7
$y = -x - 7$

Write an equation of the line shown in each graph.

4.
$y = 2x - 2$

5.
$y = -x + 3$

6.
$y = \dfrac{3}{4}x - 5$

Graph each equation.

7. $y = 2x + 1$

8. $y = -3x + 2$

9. $y = -x - 1$

© Glencoe/McGraw-Hill   293   *Glencoe Algebra 1*

NAME _____ DATE _____ PERIOD _____

5-3 Study Guide and Intervention *(continued)*

Slope-Intercept Form

Model Real-World Data

Example **MEDIA** Since 1997, the number of cable TV systems has decreased by an average rate of 121 systems per year. There were 10,943 systems in 1997.

a. Write a linear equation to find the average number of cable systems in any year after 1997.

The rate of change is -121 systems per year. In the first year, the number of systems was 10,943. Let $N =$ the number of cable TV systems. Let $x =$ the number of years after 1997.
An equation is $N = -121x + 10,943$.

b. Graph the equation.

The graph of $N = -121x + 10,943$ is a line that passes through the point at $(0, 10,943)$ and has a slope of -121.

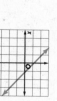

Cable TV Systems

Source: *The World Almanac*

c. Find the approximate number of cable TV systems in 2000.

$N = -121x + 10,943$ Original equation
$N = -121(3) + 10,943$ Replace x with 3.
$N = 10,580$ Simplify.

There were about 10,580 cable TV systems in 2000.

Exercises

ENTERTAINMENT In 1995, 65.7% of all households with TVs in the U.S. subscribed to cable TV. Between 1995 and 1999, the percent increased by about 0.6% each year.

1. Write an equation to find the percent P of households that subscribed to cable TV for any year x between 1995 and 1999.
$P = 0.6x + 65.7$

2. Graph the equation on the grid at the right.

Percent of Households with TV Having Cable

Source: *The World Almanac*

3. Find the percent that subscribed to cable TV in 1999. 68.1%

POPULATION The population of the United States is projected to be 300 million by the year 2010. Between 2010 and 2050, the population is expected to increase by about 2.5 million per year.

4. Write an equation to find the population P in any year x between 2010 and 2050. $P = 2,500,000x + 300,000,000$

5. Graph the equation on the grid at the right.

Projected United States Population

Source: *The World Almanac*

6. Find the population in 2050. about 400,000,000

© Glencoe/McGraw-Hill   294   *Glencoe Algebra 1*

Lesson 5-3

Practice (Average)

NAME _____ DATE _____ PERIOD _____

5-3 Practice (Average)
Slope-Intercept Form

Write an equation of the line with the given slope and y-intercept.

1. slope: $\frac{1}{4}$, y-intercept: 3 $y = \frac{1}{4}x + 3$

2. slope: $\frac{3}{2}$, y-intercept: -4 $y = \frac{3}{2}x - 4$

3. slope: 1.5, y-intercept: -1 $y = 1.5x - 1$

4. slope: -2.5, y-intercept: 3.5 $y = -2.5x + 3.5$

Write an equation of the line shown in each graph.

5.
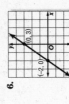
$y = \frac{2}{5}x + 2$

6.
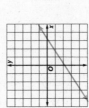
$y = \frac{3}{2}x + 3$

7.

$y = -\frac{2}{3}x - 2$

Graph each equation.

8. $y = -\frac{1}{2}x + 2$
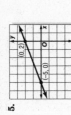

9. $3y = 2x - 6$
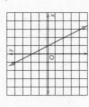

10. $6x + 3y = 6$

Write a linear equation in slope-intercept form to model each situation.

11. A computer technician charges $75 for a consultation plus $35 per hour. $C = 35h + 75$

12. The population of Pine Bluff is 6791 and is decreasing at the rate of 7 per year.
$P = -7t + 6791$

WRITING For Exercises 13-15, use the following information.
Carla has already written 10 pages of a novel. She plans to write 15 additional pages per month until she is finished.

13. Write an equation to find the total number of pages P written after any number of months m. $P = 10 + 15m$

14. Graph the equation on the grid at the right.
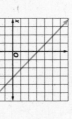
Carla's Novel

15. Find the total number of pages written after 5 months. 85

© Glencoe/McGraw-Hill   296   Glencoe Algebra 1

Lesson 5-3

Skills Practice

NAME _____ DATE _____ PERIOD _____

5-3 Skills Practice
Slope-Intercept Form

Write an equation of the line with the given slope and y-intercept.

1. slope: 5, y-intercept: -3 $y = 5x - 3$

2. slope: -2, y-intercept: 7 $y = -2x + 7$

3. slope: -6, y-intercept: -2 $y = -6x - 2$

4. slope: 7, y-intercept: 1 $y = 7x + 1$

5. slope: 3, y-intercept: 2 $y = 3x + 2$

6. slope: -4, y-intercept: -9 $y = -4x - 9$

7. slope: 1, y-intercept: -12 $y = x - 12$

8. slope: 0, y-intercept: 8 $y = 8$

Write an equation of the line shown in each graph.

9.
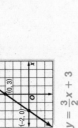
$y = 2x - 3$

10.

$y = -3x + 2$

11.

$y = -x - 1$

Graph each equation.

12. $y = x + 4$
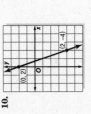

13. $y = -2x - 1$
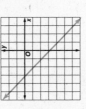

14. $x + y = -3$
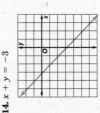

Write a linear equation in slope-intercept form to model each situation.

15. A video store charges $10 for a rental card plus $2 per rental.
$C = 2r + 10$

16. A Norfolk pine is 18 inches tall and grows at a rate of 1.5 feet per year.
$H = 1.5t + 1.5$

17. A Cairn terrier weighs 30 pounds and is on a special diet to lose 2 pounds per month.
$W = -2m + 30$

18. An airplane at an altitude of 3000 feet descends at a rate of 500 feet per mile.
$A = -500m + 3000$

© Glencoe/McGraw-Hill   295   Glencoe Algebra 1

© Glencoe/McGraw-Hill   A9   Glencoe Algebra 1

Answers

5-3 Reading to Learn Mathematics

Slope-Intercept Form

Pre-Activity **How is a y-intercept related to a flat fee?**

Read the introduction to Lesson 5-3 at the top of page 272 in your textbook.

• What point on the graph shows that the flat fee is $5.00? **(0, 5)**

• How does the rate of $0.10 per minute relate to the graph?
It is the slope.

Reading the Lesson

1. Fill in the boxes with the correct words to describe what m and b represent.

$$y = mx + b$$

slope   y-intercept

2. What are the slope and y-intercept of a vertical line?
The slope is undefined, and there is no y-intercept.

3. What are the slope and y-intercept of a horizontal line?
The slope is 0, and the y-intercept is where it crosses the y-axis.

4. Read the problem. Then answer each part of the exercise.

A ruby-throated hummingbird weighs about 0.6 gram at birth and gains weight at a rate of about 0.2 gram per day until fully grown.

a. Write a verbal equation to show how the words are related to finding the average weight of a ruby-throated hummingbird at any given week. Use the words *weight at birth, rate of growth, weight,* and *weeks after birth.* Below the equation, fill in any values you know and put a question mark under the items that you do not know.

weight	=	rate of growth	×	weeks after birth	+	weight at birth
?		0.2		?		0.6

b. Define what variables to use for the unknown quantities. **Sample answer: Let** W **be the weight at any time and** t **be the number of weeks after birth.**

c. Use the variables you defined and what you know from the problem to write an equation. $W = 0.2t + 0.6$

Helping You Remember

5. One way to remember something is to explain it to another person. Write how you would explain to someone the process for using the y-intercept and slope to graph a linear equation. **On the y-axis, plot the point for the y-intercept. Then use the rise-over-run definition of slope to determine how far up or down and right or left the next point is from the first.**

5-3 Enrichment

Relating Slope-Intercept Form and Standard Forms

You have learned that slope can be defined in terms of $\dfrac{\text{rise}}{\text{run}}$ or $\dfrac{y_2 - y_1}{x_2 - x_1}$.

Another definition can be found from the standard from of a linear equation. Standard form is $Ax + By = C$, where A, B, and C are integers, $A \geq 0$, and A and B are not both zero.

1. Solve $Ax + By = C$ for y. Your answer should be written in slope-intercept form.

$$y = -\frac{A}{B}x + \frac{C}{B}$$

2. Use the slope-intercept equation you wrote in Exercise 1 to write expressions for the slope and the y-intercept in terms of A, B, and C.

$$m = -\frac{A}{B},\ b = \frac{C}{B}$$

Use the expressions in Exercise 2 above to find the slope and y-intercept of each equation.

3. $2x + y = -4$

$$m = -2,\ b = -4$$

4. $4x + 3y = 24$

$$m = -\frac{4}{3},\ b = 8$$

5. $4x + 6y = -36$

$$m = -\frac{2}{3},\ b = -6$$

6. $x - 3y = -27$

$$m = \frac{1}{3},\ b = 9$$

7. $x - 2y = 6$

$$m = \frac{1}{2},\ b = -3$$

8. $4y = 20$

$$m = 0,\ b = 5$$

Lesson 5-3

Answers (Lesson 5-4)

5-4 Study Guide and Intervention
Writing Equations in Slope-Intercept Form

Write an Equation Given the Slope and One Point

Example 1 Write an equation of a line that passes through $(-4, 2)$ with slope 3.

The line has slope 3. To find the y-intercept, replace m with 3 and (x, y) with $(-4, 2)$ in the slope-intercept form. Then solve for b.

$y = mx + b$ Slope-intercept form
$2 = 3(-4) + b$ $m = 3, y = 2,$ and $x = -4$
$2 = -12 + b$ Multiply.
$14 = b$ Add 12 to each side.

Therefore, the equation is $y = 3x + 14$.

Example 2 Write an equation of the line that passes through $(-2, -1)$ with slope $\frac{1}{4}$.

The line has slope $\frac{1}{4}$. Replace m with $\frac{1}{4}$ and (x, y) with $(-2, -1)$ in the slope-intercept form.

$y = mx + b$ Slope-intercept form
$-1 = \frac{1}{4}(-2) + b$ $m = \frac{1}{4}, y = -1,$ and $x = -2$
$-1 = -\frac{1}{2} + b$ Multiply.
$-\frac{1}{2} = b$ Add $\frac{1}{2}$ to each side.

Therefore, the equation is $y = \frac{1}{4}x - \frac{1}{2}$.

Exercises

Write an equation of the line that passes through each point with the given slope.

1. $y = 2x - 1$
2. $y = -2x$
3. $y = \frac{1}{2}x + 3$

4. $(8, 2), m = -\frac{3}{4}$ $y = -\frac{3}{4}x + 8$
5. $(-1, -3), m = 5$ $y = 5x + 2$
6. $(4, -5), m = -\frac{1}{2}$ $y = -\frac{1}{2}x - 3$

7. $(-5, 4), m = 0$ $y = 4$
8. $(2, 2), m = \frac{1}{2}$ $y = \frac{1}{2}x + 1$
9. $(1, -4), m = -6$ $y = -6x + 2$

10. Write an equation of a line that passes through the y-intercept -3 with slope 2. $y = 2x - 3$
11. Write an equation of a line that passes through the x-intercept 4 with slope -3. $y = -3x + 12$
12. Write an equation of a line that passes through the point $(0, 350)$ with slope $\frac{1}{5}$. $y = \frac{1}{5}x + 350$

299 Glencoe Algebra 1
© Glencoe/McGraw-Hill

5-4 Study Guide and Intervention (continued)
Writing Equations in Slope-Intercept Form

Write an Equation Given Two Points

Example Write an equation of the line that passes through $(1, 2)$ and $(3, -2)$.

Find the slope m. To find the y-intercept, replace m with its computed value and (x, y) with $(1, 2)$ in the slope-intercept form. Then solve for b.

$m = \frac{y_2 - y_1}{x_2 - x_1}$ Slope formula
$m = \frac{-2 - 2}{3 - 1}$ $y_2 = -2, y_1 = 2, x_2 = 3, x_1 = 1$
$m = -2$ Simplify.

$y = mx + b$ Slope-intercept form
$2 = -2(1) + b$ Replace m with -2, y with 2, and x with 1.
$2 = -2 + b$ Multiply.
$4 = b$ Add 2 to each side.

Therefore, the equation is $y = -2x + 4$.

Exercises

Write an equation of the line that passes through each pair of points.

1. $y = 4x - 3$
2. $y = -x + 4$
3. $y = \frac{1}{3}x + 1$

4. $(-1, 6), (7, -10)$ $y = -2x + 4$
5. $(0, 2), (1, 7)$ $y = 5x + 2$
6. $(6, -25), (-1, 3)$ $y = -4x - 1$

7. $(-2, -1), (2, 11)$ $y = 3x + 5$
8. $(10, -1), (4, 2)$ $y = -\frac{1}{2}x + 4$
9. $(-14, -2), (7, 7)$ $y = \frac{3}{7}x + 4$

10. Write an equation of a line that passes through the x-intercept 4 and y-intercept -2. $y = \frac{1}{2}x - 2$
11. Write an equation of a line that passes through the x-intercept -3 and y-intercept 5. $y = \frac{5}{3}x + 5$
12. Write an equation of a line that passes through $(0, 16)$ and $(-10, 0)$. $y = \frac{8}{5}x + 16$

300 Glencoe Algebra 1
© Glencoe/McGraw-Hill

Answers

A11 © Glencoe/McGraw-Hill Glencoe Algebra 1

Left Worksheet

5-4 Skills Practice

Writing Equations in Slope-Intercept Form

Write an equation of the line that passes through each point with the given slope.

1.

$y = -3x + 1$

2.

$y = x - 3$

3.

$y = 2x + 4$

4. $(1, 9), m = 4$
$y = 4x + 5$

5. $(4, 2), m = -2$
$y = -2x + 10$

6. $(2, -2), m = 3$
$y = 3x - 8$

7. $(3, 0), m = 5$
$y = 5x - 15$

8. $(-3, -2), m = 2$
$y = 2x + 4$

9. $(-5, 4), m = -4$
$y = -4x - 16$

Write an equation of the line that passes through each pair of points.

10.

$y = -x + 1$

11.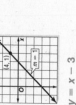

$y = 2x - 1$

12.

$y = -2x + 3$

13. $(1, 3), (-3, -5)$
$y = 2x + 1$

14. $(1, 4), (6, -1)$
$y = -x + 5$

15. $(1, -1), (3, 5)$
$y = 3x - 4$

16. $(-2, 4), (0, 6)$
$y = x + 6$

17. $(3, 3), (1, -3)$
$y = 3x - 6$

18. $(-1, 6), (3, -2)$
$y = -2x + 4$

Write an equation of the line that has each pair of intercepts.

19. x-intercept: -3, y-intercept: 6
$y = 2x + 6$

20. x-intercept: 3, y-intercept: 3
$y = -x + 3$

21. x-intercept: 1, y-intercept: 2
$y = -2x + 2$

22. x-intercept: 2, y-intercept: -4
$y = 2x - 4$

23. x-intercept: -4, y-intercept: -8
$y = -2x - 8$

24. x-intercept: -1, y-intercept: 4
$y = 4x + 4$

Right Worksheet

5-4 Practice (Average)

Writing Equations in Slope-Intercept Form

Write an equation of the line that passes through each point with the given slope.

1.

$y = 3x - 1$

2.

$y = -2x - 2$

3.

$y = -x - 4$

4. $(-5, 4), m = -3$
$y = -3x - 11$

5. $(4, 3), m = \frac{1}{2}$
$y = \frac{1}{2}x + 1$

6. $(1, -5), m = -\frac{3}{2}$
$y = -\frac{3}{2}x - \frac{7}{2}$

Write an equation of the line that passes through each pair of points.

7.

$y = x - 6$

8.

$y = -x + 5$

9.

$y = -2x - 5$

10. $(0, -4), (5, -4)$
$y = -4$

11. $(-4, -2), (4, 0)$
$y = \frac{1}{4}x - 1$

12. $(-2, -3), (4, 5)$
$y = \frac{4}{3}x - \frac{1}{3}$

13. $(0, 1), (5, 3)$
$y = \frac{2}{5}x + 1$

14. $(-3, 0), (1, -6)$
$y = -\frac{3}{2}x - \frac{9}{2}$

15. $(1, 0), (5, -1)$
$y = -\frac{1}{4}x + \frac{1}{4}$

Write an equation of the line that has each pair of intercepts.

16. x-intercept: 2, y-intercept: -5
$y = \frac{5}{2}x - 5$

17. x-intercept: 2, y-intercept: 10
$y = -5x + 10$

18. x-intercept: -2, y-intercept: 1
$y = \frac{1}{2}x + 1$

19. x-intercept: -4, y-intercept: -3
$y = -\frac{3}{4}x - 3$

20. **DANCE LESSONS** The cost for 7 dance lessons is $82. The cost for 11 lessons is $122. Write a linear equation to find the total cost C for ℓ lessons. Then use the equation to find the cost of 4 lessons. $C = 10\ell + 12$; $52

21. **WEATHER** It is 76°F at the 6000-foot level of a mountain, and 49°F at the 12,000-foot level of the mountain. Write a linear equation to find the temperature T at an elevation e on the mountain, where e is in thousands of feet. $T = -4.5e + 103$

NAME _____ DATE _____ PERIOD _____

5-4 Reading to Learn Mathematics

Writing Equations in Slope-Intercept Form

Pre-Activity How can slope-intercept form be used to make predictions?

Read the introduction to Lesson 5-4 at the top of page 280 in your textbook.

- What is the rate of change per year? **about 2000 per year**
- Study the pattern on the graph. How would you find the population in 1997? **Add 2000 to the 1996 population, which gives 179,000.**

Reading the Lesson

1. Suppose you are given that a line goes through (2, 5) and has a slope of −2. Use this information to complete the following equation.

$y = mx + b$

$5 = \boxed{-2} \cdot \boxed{2} + \boxed{b}$

2. What must you first do if you are not given the slope in the problem? **Use the information given (two points) to find the slope.**

3. What is the first step in answering any standardized test practice question? **Read the problem.**

4. What are four steps you can use in solving a word problem? **Explore, Plan, Solve, Examine**

5. Define the term *linear extrapolation*. **Linear extrapolation means using a linear equation to predict values that are outside the two given data points.**

Helping You Remember

6. In your own words, explain how you would answer a question that asks you to write the slope-intercept form of an equation. **Sample answer: Determine what information you are given. If you have a point and the slope, you can substitute the x- and y-values and the slope into $y = mx + b$ to find the value of b. Then use the values of m and b to write the equation. If you have two points, use them to find the slope, and then use the method for a point and the slope.**

NAME _____ DATE _____ PERIOD _____

5-4 Enrichment

Celsius and Kelvin Temperatures

If you blow up a balloon and put it in the refrigerator, the balloon will shrink as the temperature of the air in the balloon decreases.

The volume of a certain gas is measured at 30° Celsius. The temperature is decreased and the volume is measured again.

Temperature (t)	Volume (V)
30°C	202 mL
21°C	196 mL
0°C	182 mL
−12°C	174 mL
−27°C	164 mL

1. Graph this table on the coordinate plane provided below.

2. Find the equation of the line that passes through the points you graphed in Exercise 1.

$v = \frac{2}{3}t + 182$

3. Use the equation you found in Exercise 2 to find the temperature that would give a volume of zero. This temperature is the lowest one possible and is called *absolute zero*.

−273°C

4. In 1848, Lord Kelvin proposed a new temperature scale with 0 being assigned to absolute zero. The size of the degree chosen was the same size as the Celsius degree. Change each of the Celsius temperatures in the table above to degrees Kelvin.

303°, 294°, 273°, 261°, 246°

Answers

Lesson 5-4

Answers (Lesson 5-5)

Page 305

NAME _____ DATE _____ PERIOD _____

5-5 Study Guide and Intervention

Writing Equations in Point-Slope Form

Point-Slope Form

Point-Slope Form	$y - y_1 = m(x - x_1)$, where (x_1, y_1) is a given point on a nonvertical line and m is the slope of the line

Example 1 Write the point-slope form of an equation for a line that passes through (6, 1) and has a slope of $-\frac{5}{2}$.

$y - y_1 = m(x - x_1)$ Point-slope form
$y - 1 = -\frac{5}{2}(x - 6)$ $m = -\frac{5}{2}; (x_1, y_1) = (6, 1)$

Therefore, the equation is $y - 1 = -\frac{5}{2}(x - 6)$.

Example 2 Write the point-slope form of an equation for a horizontal line that passes through (4, −1).

$y - y_1 = m(x - x_1)$ Point-slope form
$y - (-1) = 0(x - 4)$ $m = 0; (x_1, y_1) = (4, -1)$
$y + 1 = 0$ Simplify.

Therefore, the equation is $y + 1 = 0$.

Exercises

Write the point-slope form of an equation for a line that passes through each point with the given slope.

1.
$y - 1 = x - 4$

2.
$y - 2 = 0$

3.
$y + 3 = -2(x - 2)$

4. (2, 1), $m = 4$
$y - 1 = 4(x - 2)$

5. (−7, 2), $m = 6$
$y - 2 = 6(x + 7)$

6. (8, 3), $m = 1$
$y - 3 = x - 8$

7. (−6, 7), $m = 0$
$y - 7 = 0$

8. (4, 9), $m = \frac{3}{4}$
$y - 9 = \frac{3}{4}(x - 4)$

9. (−4, −5), $m = -\frac{1}{2}$
$y + 5 = -\frac{1}{2}(x + 4)$

10. Write the point-slope form of an equation for the horizontal line that passes through (4, −2). $y + 2 = 0$

11. Write the point-slope form of an equation for the horizontal line that passes through (−5, 6). $y - 6 = 0$

12. Write the point-slope form of an equation for the horizontal line that passes through (5, 0). $y = 0$

© Glencoe/McGraw-Hill 305 *Glencoe Algebra 1*

Page 306

NAME _____ DATE _____ PERIOD _____

5-5 Study Guide and Intervention (continued)

Writing Equations in Point-Slope Form

Forms of Linear Equations

Slope-Intercept Form	$y = mx + b$	m = slope; b = y-intercept
Point-Slope Form	$y - y_1 = m(x - x_1)$	m = slope; (x_1, y_1) is a given point.
Standard Form	$Ax + By = C$	A and B are not both zero. Usually A is nonnegative and A, B, and C are integers whose greatest common factor is 1.

Example 1 Write $y + 5 = \frac{2}{3}(x - 6)$ in standard form.

$y + 5 = \frac{2}{3}(x - 6)$ Original equation
$3(y + 5) = 3\left(\frac{2}{3}\right)(x - 6)$ Multiply each side by 3.
$3y + 15 = 2(x - 6)$ Distributive Property
$3y + 15 = 2x - 12$ Distributive Property
$3y = 2x - 27$ Subtract 15 from each side.
$-2x + 3y = -27$ Add −2x to each side.
$2x - 3y = 27$ Multiply each side by −1.

Therefore, the standard form of the equation is $2x - 3y = 27$.

Example 2 Write $y - 2 = -\frac{1}{4}(x - 8)$ in slope-intercept form.

$y - 2 = -\frac{1}{4}(x - 8)$ Original equation
$y - 2 = -\frac{1}{4}x + 2$ Distributive Property
$y = -\frac{1}{4}x + 4$ Add 2 to each side.

Therefore, the slope-intercept form of the equation is $y = -\frac{1}{4}x + 4$.

Exercises

Write each equation in standard form.

1. $y + 2 = -3(x - 1)$
$3x + y = 1$

2. $y - 1 = -\frac{1}{3}(x - 6)$
$x + 3y = 9$

3. $y + 2 = \frac{2}{3}(x - 9)$
$2x - 3y = 24$

4. $y + 3 = -(x - 5)$
$x + y = 2$

5. $y - 4 = \frac{5}{3}(x + 3)$
$5x - 3y = -27$

6. $y + 4 = -\frac{2}{5}(x - 1)$
$2x + 5y = -18$

Write each equation in slope-intercept form.

7. $y + 4 = 4(x - 2)$
$y = 4x - 12$

8. $y - 5 = \frac{1}{3}(x - 6)$
$y = \frac{1}{3}x + 3$

9. $y - 8 = -\frac{1}{4}(x + 8)$
$y = -\frac{1}{4}x + 6$

10. $y - 6 = 3\left(x - \frac{1}{3}\right)$
$y = 3x + 5$

11. $y + 4 = -2(x + 5)$
$y = -2x - 14$

12. $y + \frac{5}{2} = \frac{1}{2}(x - 2)$
$y = \frac{1}{2}x - \frac{8}{3}$

© Glencoe/McGraw-Hill 306 *Glencoe Algebra 1*

Lesson 5-5

© Glencoe/McGraw-Hill   **A14**   *Glencoe Algebra 1*

Answers (Lesson 5-5)

5-5 Practice (Average)

Writing Equations in Point-Slope Form

Write the point-slope form of an equation for a line that passes through each point with the given slope.

1. $(2, 2), m = -3$
$y - 2 = -3(x - 2)$

2. $(1, -6), m = -1$
$y + 6 = -(x - 1)$

3. $(-3, -4), m = 0$
$y + 4 = 0$

4. $(1, 3), m = -\frac{3}{4}$
$y - 3 = -\frac{3}{4}(x - 1)$

5. $(-8, 5), m = -\frac{2}{5}$
$y - 5 = -\frac{2}{5}(x + 8)$

6. $(3, -3), m = \frac{1}{3}$
$y + 3 = \frac{1}{3}(x - 3)$

Write each equation in standard form.

7. $y - 11 = 3(x - 2)$
$3x - y = -5$

8. $y - 10 = -(x - 2)$
$x + y = 12$

9. $y + 7 = 2(x + 5)$
$2x - y = -3$

10. $y - 5 = \frac{3}{2}(x + 4)$
$3x - 2y = -22$

11. $y + 2 = -\frac{3}{4}(x + 1)$
$3x + 4y = -11$

12. $y - 6 = \frac{4}{3}(x - 3)$
$4x - 3y = -6$

13. $y + 4 = 1.5(x + 2)$
$3x - 2y = 2$

14. $y - 3 = -2.4(x - 5)$
$12x + 5y = 75$

15. $y - 4 = 2.5(x + 3)$
$5x - 2y = -23$

Write each equation in slope-intercept form.

16. $y + 2 = 4(x + 2)$
$y = 4x + 6$

17. $y + 1 = -7(x + 1)$
$y = -7x - 8$

18. $y - 3 = -5(x + 12)$
$y = -5x - 57$

19. $y - 5 = \frac{3}{2}(x + 4)$
$y = \frac{3}{2}x + 11$

20. $y - \frac{1}{4} = -3\left(x + \frac{1}{4}\right)$
$y = -3x - \frac{1}{2}$

21. $y - \frac{2}{3} = -2\left(x - \frac{1}{4}\right)$
$y = -2x + \frac{7}{6}$

CONSTRUCTION For Exercises 22–24, use the following information.
A construction company charges $15 per hour for debris removal, plus a one-time fee for the use of a trash dumpster. The total fee for 9 hours of service is $195.

22. Write the point-slope form of an equation to find the total fee y for any number of hours x.
$y - 195 = 15(x - 9)$

23. Write the equation in slope-intercept form. $y = 15x + 60$

24. What is the fee for the use of a trash dumpster? **$60**

MOVING For Exercises 25–27, use the following information.
There is a set daily fee for renting a moving truck, plus a charge of $0.50 per mile driven. It costs $64 to rent the truck on a day when it is driven 48 miles.

25. Write the point-slope form of an equation to find the total charge y for any number of miles x for a one-day rental. $y - 64 = 0.5(x - 48)$

26. Write the equation in slope-intercept form. $y = 0.5x + 40$

27. What is the daily fee? **$40**

Lesson 5-5

5-5 Skills Practice

Writing Equations in Point-Slope Form

Write the point-slope form of an equation for a line that passes through each point with the given slope.

1.

$y + 2 = 3(x + 1)$

2.

$y + 2 = -(x - 1)$

3.

$y + 3 = 0$

4. $(3, 1), m = 0$
$y - 1 = 0$

5. $(-4, 6), m = 8$
$y - 6 = 8(x + 4)$

6. $(1, -3), m = -4$
$y + 3 = -4(x - 1)$

7. $(4, -6), m = 1$
$y + 6 = x - 4$

8. $(3, 3), m = \frac{4}{3}$
$y - 3 = \frac{4}{3}(x - 3)$

9. $(-5, -1), m = -\frac{5}{4}$
$y + 1 = -\frac{5}{4}(x + 5)$

Write each equation in standard form.

10. $y + 1 = x + 2$
$x - y = -1$

11. $y + 9 = -3(x - 2)$
$3x + y = -3$

12. $y - 7 = 4(x + 4)$
$4x - y = -23$

13. $y - 4 = -(x - 1)$
$x + y = 5$

14. $y - 6 = 4(x + 3)$
$4x - y = -18$

15. $y + 5 = -5(x - 3)$
$5x + y = 10$

16. $y - 10 = -2(x - 3)$
$2x + y = 16$

17. $y - 2 = -\frac{1}{2}(x - 4)$
$x + 2y = 8$

18. $y + 11 = \frac{1}{3}(x + 3)$
$x - 3y = 30$

Write each equation in slope-intercept form.

19. $y - 4 = 3(x - 2)$
$y = 3x - 2$

20. $y + 2 = -(x + 4)$
$y = -x - 6$

21. $y - 6 = -2(x + 2)$
$y = -2x + 2$

22. $y + 1 = -5(x - 3)$
$y = -5x + 14$

23. $y - 3 = 6(x - 1)$
$y = 6x - 3$

24. $y - 8 = 3(x + 5)$
$y = 3x + 23$

25. $y - 2 = \frac{1}{2}(x + 6)$
$y = \frac{1}{2}x + 5$

26. $y + 1 = -\frac{1}{3}(x + 9)$
$y = -\frac{1}{3}x - 4$

27. $y - \frac{1}{2} = x + \frac{1}{2}$
$y = x + 1$

Answers

Left panel

5-5 **Reading to Learn Mathematics**

Writing Equations in Point-Slope Form

Pre-Activity **How can you use the slope formula to write an equation of a line?**

Read the introduction to Lesson 5-5 at the top of page 286 in your textbook.

Note that in the final equation there is a value subtracted from x and from y. What are these values?

The value subtracted from x is the x-coordinate of the given point. The value subtracted from y is the y-coordinate of the given point.

Reading the Lesson

1. In the formula $y - y_1 = m(x - x_1)$, what do x_1 and y_1 represent?

x_1 and y_1 represent the coordinates of any given point on the graph of the line.

2. Complete the chart below by listing three forms of equations. Then write the formula for each form. Finally, write three examples of equations in those forms. Sample examples are given.

Form of Equation	Formula	Example
slope-intercept	$y = mx + b$	$y = 3x + 2$
point-slope	$y - y_1 = m(x - x_1)$	$y - 2 = 4(x + 3)$
standard	$Ax + By = C$	$3x - 5y = 15$

3. Refer to Example 5 on page 288 of your textbook. What do you think the *hypotenuse* of a right triangle is? Sample answers: The hypotenuse is the longest side of the right triangle. The hypotenuse is the side opposite the right angle in a right triangle.

Helping You Remember

4. Suppose you could not remember all three formulas listed in the table above. Which of the forms would you concentrate on for writing linear equations? Explain why you chose that form. Sample answer: Point-slope form; the slope-intercept form can be written from the point-slope form. This is so because the y-intercept lets you write the coordinates of the point where the line crosses the y-axis. You can use that point as the given point in the point-slope formula.

Lesson 5-5

Right panel

5-5 **Enrichment**

Collinearity

You have learned how to find the slope between two points on a line. Does it matter which two points you use? How does your choice of points affect the slope-intercept form of the equation of the line?

1. Choose three different pairs of points from the graph at the right. Write the slope-intercept form of the line using each pair.

$y = 1x + 1$

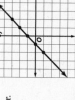

2. How are the equations related?

They are the same.

3. What conclusion can you draw from your answers to Exercises 1 and 2?

The equation of a line is the same no matter which two points you choose.

When points are contained in the same line, they are said to be **collinear**. Even though points may *look* like they form a straight line when connected, it does not mean that they actually do. By checking pairs of points on a line you can determine whether the line represents a linear relationship.

4. Choose several pairs of points from the graph at the right and write the slope-intercept form of the line using each pair.

$y = 1x + 0; y = 2x - 2; y = 2x + 1$

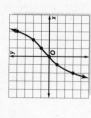

5. What conclusion can you draw from your equations in Exercise 4? Is this a straight line?

The points are not collinear. This is not a straight line.

5-6 Study Guide and Intervention
Geometry: Parallel and Perpendicular Lines

Parallel Lines Two nonvertical lines are **parallel** if they have the same slope. All vertical lines are parallel.

Example **Write the slope-intercept form for an equation of the line that passes through $(-1, 6)$ and is parallel to the graph of $y = 2x + 12$.**

A line parallel to $y = 2x + 12$ has the same slope, 2. Replace m with 2 and (x_1, y_1) with $(-1, 6)$ in the point-slope form.

$y - y_1 = m(x - x_1)$ Point-slope form.
$y - 6 = 2(x - (-1))$ $m = 2; (x_1, y_1) = (-1, 6)$
$y - 6 = 2(x + 1)$ Simplify.
$y - 6 = 2x + 2$ Distributive Property
$y = 2x + 8$ Slope-intercept form

Therefore, the equation is $y = 2x + 8$.

Exercises

Write the slope-intercept form for an equation of the line that passes through the given point and is parallel to the graph of each equation.

1. $y = x - 4$

2. $y = -\frac{1}{2}x + 3$

3. $y = \frac{4}{3}x + 7$

4. $(-2, 2), y = 4x - 2$
$y = 4x + 10$

5. $(6, 4), y = \frac{1}{3}x + 1$
$y = \frac{1}{3}x + 2$

6. $(4, -2), y = -2x + 3$
$y = -2x + 6$

7. $(-2, 4), y = -3x + 10$
$y = -3x - 2$

8. $(-1, 6), 3x + y = 12$
$y = -3x + 3$

9. $(4, -6), x + 2y = 5$
$y = -\frac{1}{2}x - 4$

10. Find an equation of the line that has a y-intercept of 2 that is parallel to the graph of the line $4x + 2y = 8$. $y = -2x + 2$

11. Find an equation of the line that has a y-intercept of -1 that is parallel to the graph of the line $x - 3y = 6$. $y = \frac{1}{3}x - 1$

12. Find an equation of the line that has a y-intercept of -4 that is parallel to the graph of the line $y = 6$. $y = -4$

5-6 Study Guide and Intervention (continued)
Geometry: Parallel and Perpendicular Lines

Perpendicular Lines Two lines are **perpendicular** if their slopes are negative reciprocals of each other. Vertical and horizontal lines are perpendicular.

Example **Write the slope-intercept form for an equation that passes through $(-4, 2)$ and is perpendicular to the graph of $2x - 3y = 9$.**

Find the slope of $2x - 3y = 9$.
$2x - 3y = 9$ Original equation
$-3y = -2x + 9$ Subtract $2x$ from each side.
$y = \frac{2}{3}x - 3$ Divide each side by -3.

The slope of $y = \frac{2}{3}x - 3$ is $\frac{2}{3}$. So, the slope of the line passing through $(-4, 2)$ that is perpendicular to this line is the negative reciprocal of $\frac{2}{3}$, or $-\frac{3}{2}$. Use the point-slope form to find the equation.

$y - y_1 = m(x - x_1)$ Point-slope form
$y - 2 = -\frac{3}{2}(x - (-4))$ $m = -\frac{3}{2}; (x_1, y_1) = (-4, 2)$
$y - 2 = -\frac{3}{2}(x + 4)$ Simplify.
$y - 2 = -\frac{3}{2}x - 6$ Distributive Property
$y = -\frac{3}{2}x - 4$ Slope-intercept form

Exercises

Write the slope-intercept form for an equation of the line that passes through the given point and is perpendicular to the graph of each equation.

1. $(4, 2), y = \frac{1}{2}x + 1$
$y = -2x + 10$

2. $(2, -3), y = -\frac{2}{3}x + 4$
$y = \frac{3}{2}x - 6$

3. $(6, 4), y = 7x + 1$
$y = -\frac{1}{7}x + \frac{34}{7}$

4. $(-8, -7), y = -x - 8$
$y = x + 1$

5. $(6, -2), y = -3x - 6$
$y = \frac{1}{3}x - 4$

6. $(-5, -1), y = \frac{5}{2}x - 3$
$y = -\frac{2}{5}x - 3$

7. $(-9, -5), y = -3x - 1$
$y = \frac{1}{3}x - 2$

8. $(-1, 3), 2x + 4y = 12$
$y = 2x + 5$

9. $(6, -6), 3x - y = 6$
$y = -\frac{1}{3}x - 4$

10. Find an equation of the line that has a y-intercept of -2 and is perpendicular to the graph of the line $x - 2y = 5$. $y = -2x - 2$

11. Find an equation of the line that has a y-intercept of 5 and is perpendicular to the graph of the line $4x + 3y = 8$. $y = \frac{3}{4}x + 5$

Answers

Skills Practice (Left Page)

5-6 Skills Practice

Geometry: Parallel and Perpendicular Lines

Write the slope-intercept form of an equation of the line that passes through the given point and is parallel to the graph of each equation.

1. $y = 2x + 1$

2. $y = -x$

3. 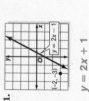 $y = \frac{1}{2}x + 3$

4. $(3, 2)$, $y = 3x + 4$
$y = 3x - 7$

5. $(-1, -2)$, $y = -3x + 5$
$y = -3x - 5$

6. $(-1, 1)$, $y = x - 4$
$y = x + 2$

7. $(1, -3)$, $y = -4x - 1$
$y = -4x + 1$

8. $(-4, 2)$, $y = x + 3$
$y = x + 6$

9. $(-4, 3)$, $y = \frac{1}{2}x + 5$
$y = \frac{1}{2}x + 5$

10. $(4, 1)$, $y = -\frac{1}{4}x + 7$
$y = -\frac{1}{4}x + 2$

11. $(-5, -1)$, $2y = 2x - 4$
$y = x + 4$

12. $(3, -1)$, $3y = x + 9$
$y = \frac{1}{3}x - 2$

Write the slope-intercept form of an equation of the line that passes through the given point and is perpendicular to the graph of each equation.

13. $(-3, -2)$, $y = x + 2$
$y = -x - 5$

14. $(4, -1)$, $y = 2x - 4$
$y = -\frac{1}{2}x + 1$

15. $(-1, -6)$, $x + 3y = 6$
$y = 3x - 3$

16. $(-4, 5)$, $y = -4x - 1$
$y = \frac{1}{4}x + 6$

17. $(-2, 3)$, $y = \frac{1}{4}x - 4$
$y = -4x - 5$

18. $(0, 0)$, $y = \frac{1}{2}x - 1$
$y = -2x$

19. $(3, -3)$, $y = \frac{3}{4}x + 5$
$y = -\frac{4}{3}x + 1$

20. $(-5, 1)$, $y = -\frac{5}{3}x - 7$
$y = \frac{3}{5}x + 4$

21. $(0, -2)$, $y = -7x + 3$
$y = \frac{1}{7}x - 2$

22. $(2, 3)$, $2x + 10y = 3$
$y = 5x - 7$

23. $(-2, 2)$, $6x + 3y = -9$
$y = \frac{1}{2}x + 3$

24. $(-4, -3)$, $8x - 2y = 16$
$y = -\frac{1}{4}x - 4$

Practice (Right Page)

5-6 Practice (Average)

Geometry: Parallel and Perpendicular Lines

Write the slope-intercept form of an equation of the line that passes through the given point and is parallel to the graph of each equation.

1. $(3, 2)$, $y = x + 5$
$y = x - 1$

2. $(-2, 5)$, $y = -4x + 2$
$y = -4x - 3$

3. $(4, -6)$, $y = -\frac{3}{4}x + 1$
$y = -\frac{3}{4}x - 3$

4. $(5, 4)$, $y = \frac{2}{5}x - 2$
$y = \frac{2}{5}x + 2$

5. $(12, 3)$, $y = \frac{4}{3}x + 5$
$y = \frac{4}{3}x - 13$

6. $(3, 1)$, $2x + y = 5$
$y = -2x + 7$

7. $(-3, 4)$, $3y = 2x - 3$
$y = \frac{2}{3}x + 6$

8. $(-1, -2)$, $3x - y = 5$
$y = 3x + 1$

9. $(-8, 2)$, $5x - 4y = 1$
$y = \frac{5}{4}x + 12$

10. $(-1, -4)$, $9x + 3y = 8$
$y = -3x - 7$

11. $(-5, 6)$, $4x + 3y = 1$
$y = -\frac{4}{3}x - \frac{2}{3}$

12. $(3, 1)$, $2x + 5y = 7$
$y = -\frac{2}{5}x + \frac{11}{5}$

Write the slope-intercept form of an equation of the line that passes through the given point and is perpendicular to the graph of each equation.

13. $(-2, -2)$, $y = -\frac{1}{3}x + 9$
$y = 3x + 4$

14. $(-6, 5)$, $x - y = 5$
$y = -x - 1$

15. $(-4, -3)$, $4x + y = 7$
$y = \frac{1}{4}x - 2$

16. $(0, 1)$, $x + 5y = 15$
$y = 5x + 1$

17. $(2, 4)$, $x - 6y = 2$
$y = -6x + 16$

18. $(-1, -7)$, $3x + 12y = -6$
$y = 4x - 3$

19. $(-4, 1)$, $4x + 7y = 6$
$y = \frac{7}{4}x + 8$

20. $(10, 5)$, $5x + 4y = 8$
$y = \frac{4}{5}x - 3$

21. $(4, -5)$, $2x - 5y = -10$
$y = -\frac{5}{2}x + 5$

22. $(1, 1)$, $3x + 2y = -7$
$y = \frac{2}{3}x + \frac{1}{3}$

23. $(-6, -5)$, $4x + 3y = -6$
$y = \frac{3}{4}x - \frac{1}{2}$

24. $(-3, 5)$, $5x - 6y = 9$
$y = -\frac{6}{5}x + \frac{7}{5}$

25. **GEOMETRY** Quadrilateral $ABCD$ has diagonals $\overline{AC}$ and $\overline{BD}$. Determine whether $\overline{AC}$ is perpendicular to $\overline{BD}$. Explain.
Yes; they are perpendicular because their slopes are 7 and $-\frac{1}{7}$, which are negative reciprocals.

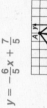

26. **GEOMETRY** Triangle ABC has vertices $A(0, 4)$, $B(1, 2)$, and $C(4, 6)$. Determine whether triangle ABC is a right triangle. Explain.
Yes; sides $\overline{AB}$ and $\overline{AC}$ are perpendicular because their slopes are -2 and $\frac{1}{2}$, which are negative reciprocals.

5-6 Enrichment

Lesson 5-6

Pencils of Lines

All of the lines that pass through a single point in the same plane are called a **pencil of lines**.

All lines with the same slope, but different intercepts, are also called a "pencil," a **pencil of parallel lines**.

Graph some of the lines in each pencil.

1. A pencil of lines through the point (1, 3)

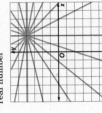

2. A pencil of lines described by $y - 4 = m(x - 2)$, where m is any real number

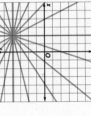

3. A pencil of lines parallel to the line $x - 2y = 7$

4. A pencil of lines described by $y = mx + 3m - 2$

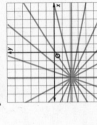

5-6 Reading to Learn Mathematics

Geometry: Parallel and Perpendicular Lines

Pre-Activity **How can you determine whether two lines are parallel?**

Read the introduction to Lesson 5-6 at the top of page 292 in your textbook.

• What is a family of graphs? **A group of graphs that have at least one characteristic in common, such as slope or *y*-intercept.**

• Do you think lines that do not appear to intersect are parallel or perpendicular? **parallel**

Reading the Lesson

1. Refer to the Key Concept box on page 292. Why does the definition use the term *nonvertical* when talking about lines with the same slope? **Vertical lines have slopes that are undefined so we cannot say they have the same slope.**

2. What is a right angle? Sample answers: **A right angle is one that measures 90°. It is an angle formed by perpendicular lines.**

3. Refer to the Key Concept box on page 293. Describe how you find the opposite reciprocal of a number. Sample answer: **The reciprocal of a given number is the number formed when you switch the numerator and denominator. Then you give it the opposite sign of the original number.**

4. Write the opposite reciprocal of each number.

a. 2 $-\frac{1}{2}$ **b.** -3 $\frac{1}{3}$ **c.** $\frac{12}{13}$ $-\frac{13}{12}$ **d.** $-\frac{1}{5}$ 5

Helping You Remember

5. One way to remember how slopes of parallel lines are related is to say "same direction, same slope." Try to think of a phrase to help you remember that perpendicular lines have slopes that are opposite reciprocals.

Sample answer: Nicely <u>right angles formed, use opposite reciprocals.</u>

Page 317

NAME _____ DATE _____ PERIOD _____

5-7 Study Guide and Intervention

Scatter Plots and Lines of Fit

Interpret Points on a Scatter Plot A scatter plot is a graph in which two sets of data are plotted as ordered pairs in a coordinate plane. If y increases as x increases, there is a **positive** correlation between x and y. If y decreases as x increases, there is a **negative** correlation between x and y. If x and y are not related, there is **no correlation**.

Example EARNINGS The graph at the right shows the amount of money Carmen earned each week and the amount she deposited in her savings account that same week. Determine whether the graph shows a positive correlation, a negative correlation, or no correlation. If there is a positive or negative correlation, describe its meaning in the situation.

The graph shows a positive correlation. The more Carmen earns, the more she saves.

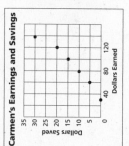
Carmen's Earnings and Savings

Exercises

Determine whether each graph shows a positive correlation, a negative correlation, or no correlation. If there is a positive correlation, describe it.

1. **Average Weekly Work Hours in U.S.**

Source: *The World Almanac*
no correlation

2. **Average Jogging Speed**
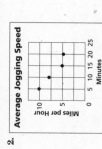
Negative correlation; as time increases, speed decreases.

3. **Growth of Investment Clubs**
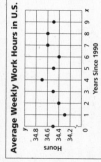
Source: *The Wall Street Journal Almanac*
Positive correlation; as the number of years increases, the number of clubs increases.

4. **Number of Mutual Funds**
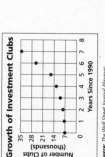
Source: *The Wall Street Journal Almanac*
Positive correlation; as the number of years increases, the number of funds increases.

Page 318

NAME _____ DATE _____ PERIOD _____

5-7 Study Guide and Intervention *(continued)*

Scatter Plots and Lines of Fit

Lines of Fit

Example The table below shows the number of students per computer in United States public schools for certain school years from 1990 to 2000.

Year	1990	1992	1994	1996	1998	2000
Students per Computer	22	18	14	10	6.1	5.4

a. Draw a scatter plot and determine what relationship exists, if any.
Since y decreases as x increases, the correlation is negative.

b. Draw a line of fit for the scatter plot.
Draw a line that passes close to most of the points. A line of fit is shown.

Students per Computer in U.S. Public Schools
Source: *The World Almanac*

c. Write the slope-intercept form of an equation for the line of fit.
The line of fit shown passes through (1993, 16) and (1999, 5.7). Find the slope.

$$m = \frac{5.7 - 16}{1999 - 1993}$$
$$m = -1.7$$

Find b in $y = -1.7x + b$.
$16 = -1.7 \cdot 1993 + b$
$3404 = b$

Therefore, an equation of a line of fit is $y = -1.7x + 3404$.

Exercises

Refer to the table for Exercises 1–3.

Years Since 1995	Hourly Wage
0	$11.43
1	$11.82
2	$12.28
3	$12.78
4	$13.24

1. Draw a scatter plot.
2. Draw a line of fit for the data.

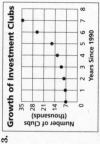
U.S. Production Workers Hourly Wage
Source: *The World Almanac*

3. Write the slope-intercept form of an equation for the line of fit.
The points (0, 11.43) and (2, 12.28) give $y = 0.425x + 11.43$ as a line of fit.

Left Panel

5-7 Skills Practice

Statistics: Scatter Plots and Lines of Fit

Determine whether each graph shows a *positive correlation*, a *negative correlation*, or *no correlation*. If there is a positive or negative correlation, describe its meaning in the situation.

1.

Calories Burned During Exercise

Calories (y-axis): 600, 500, 400, 300, 200, 100
Time (minutes) (x-axis): 0 10 20 30 40 50 60

Positive; the longer the exercise, the more Calories burned.

2.

Library Fines

Fines (dollars) (y-axis): 7, 6, 5, 4, 3, 2, 1
Books Borrowed (x-axis): 0 1 2 3 4 5 6 7 8 9 10

no correlation

3.

Weight-Lifting

Repetitions (y-axis): 14, 12, 10, 8, 6, 4, 2
Weight (pounds) (x-axis): 0 20 40 60 80 100 120 140

Negative; as weight increases, the number of repetitions decreases.

4.

Evening Newspapers

Number of Newspapers (y-axis): 1050, 1000, 950, 900, 850, 800, 750
Year (x-axis): '91 '92 '93 '94 '95 '96 '97 '98 '99

Source: *Editor & Publisher*

Negative; as the year increases, the number of evening newspapers decreases.

BASEBALL For Exercises 5–7, use the scatter plot that shows the average price of a major-league baseball ticket from 1991 to 2000.

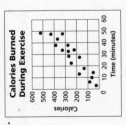

Baseball Ticket Prices

Average Price ($) (y-axis): 18, 16, 14, 12, 10, 8
Year (x-axis): '91 '92 '93 '94 '95 '96 '97 '98 '99 '00

Source: Team Marketing Report, Chicago

5. Determine what relationship, if any, exists in the data. Explain. **Positive correlation; as the year increases, the price increases.**

6. Use the points (1993, 9.60) and (1998, 13.60) to write the slope-intercept form of an equation for the line of fit shown in the scatter plot.
$y = 0.8x - 1584.8$

7. Predict the price of a ticket in 2004. **about $18.40**

© Glencoe/McGraw-Hill **319** *Glencoe Algebra 1*

Lesson 5-7

Right Panel

5-7 Practice (Average)

Statistics: Scatter Plots and Lines of Fit

Determine whether each graph shows a *positive correlation*, a *negative correlation*, or *no correlation*. If there is a positive or negative correlation, describe its meaning in the situation.

1.

Temperature versus Rainfall

Average Temperature (°F) (y-axis): 64, 60, 56, 52
Average Annual Rainfall (inches) (x-axis): 0 10 15 20 25 30 35 40 45

Source: National Oceanic and Atmospheric Administration

no correlation

2.

State Elevations

Highest Point (thousands of feet) (y-axis): 16, 12, 8, 4
Mean Elevation (feet) (x-axis): 0 1000 2000 3000

Source: U.S. Geological Survey

Positive; as the mean elevation increases, the highest point increases.

DISEASE For Exercises 3–6, use the table that shows the number of cases of mumps in the United States for the years 1995 to 1999.

U.S. Mumps Cases

Year	1995	1996	1997	1998	1999
Cases	906	751	683	666	387

Source: Centers for Disease Control and Prevention

U.S. Mumps Cases

Cases (y-axis): 1000, 800, 600, 400, 200
Year (x-axis): 0 1995 1997 1999 2001

3. Draw a scatter plot and determine what relationship, if any, exists in the data. **Negative correlation; as the year increases, the number of cases decreases.**

4. Draw a line of fit for the scatter plot. **Sample answer: Use (1996, 751), (1997, 683).**

5. Write the slope-intercept form of an equation for the line of fit. **Sample answer: $y = -68x + 136,479$**

6. Predict the number of cases in 2004. **about 207**

ZOOS For Exercises 7–10, use the table that shows the average and maximum longevity of various animals in captivity.

Longevity (years)

Avg.	12	25	15	8	35	40	41	20
Max.	47	50	40	20	70	77	61	54

Source: Walker's Mammals of the World

Animal Longevity (Years)

Maximum (y-axis): 80, 70, 60, 50, 40, 30, 20, 10
Average (x-axis): 0 5 10 15 20 25 30 35 40 45

7. Draw a scatter plot and determine what relationship, if any, exists in the data. **Positive correlation; as the average increases, the maximum increases.**

8. Draw a line of fit for the scatter plot. **Sample answer: Use (15, 40), (35, 70).**

9. Write the slope-intercept form of an equation for the line of fit. **Sample answer: $y = 1.5x + 17.5$**

10. Predict the maximum longevity for an animal with an average longevity of 33 years. **about 67 yr**

© Glencoe/McGraw-Hill **320** *Glencoe Algebra 1*

Answers (Lesson 5-7)

(Page 321)

NAME _____ DATE _____ PERIOD _____

5-7 Reading to Learn Mathematics

Statistics: Scatter Plots and Lines of Fit

Pre-Activity **How do scatter plots help identify trends in data?**

Read the introduction to Lesson 5-7 at the top of page 298 in your textbook.

- What does the phrase *linear relationship* mean to you? **Sample answer: It means that when you graph the data points on a coordinate grid, the points all lie on or close to a line that you could draw on the grid.**

- Write three ordered pairs that fit the description *as x increases, y decreases*. **Sample answer: {(2, 5), (3, 3), (4, 1)}**

Reading the Lesson

1. Look up the word *scatter* in a dictionary. How does this definition compare to the term *scatter plot?* One definition states "to occur or fall irregularly or at random." The points in a scatter plots usually do not follow an exact linear pattern, but fall irregularly on the coordinate plane.

2. What is a *line of fit?* How many data points fall on the line of fit? A line of fit shows the trend of the data. It is impossible to say how many data points may fall on a line of fit—maybe several, maybe none.

3. What is *linear interpolation?* How can you distinguish it from linear *extrapolation?* Linear interpolation is the process of predicting a *y*-value for a given *x*-value that lies between the least and greatest *x*-values in the data set. "Inter-" means between and "extra-" means beyond. If the *x*-value is between the extremes of the *x*-values in the data set, you say interpolation; if the *x*-value is less than or greater than the extremes, you say extrapolation.

Helping You Remember

4. How can you remember whether a set of data points shows a positive correlation or a negative correlation? If it looks like a line of fit for the points would have a positive slope, there is a positive correlation. If it looks like a line of fit would have a negative slope, there is a negative correlation.

© Glencoe/McGraw-Hill

321

Glencoe Algebra 1

(Page 322)

NAME _____ DATE _____ PERIOD _____

5-7 Enrichment

Latitude and Temperature

The *latitude* of a place on Earth is the measure of its distance from the equator. What do you think is the relationship between a city's latitude and its January temperature? At the right is a table containing the latitudes and January mean temperatures for fifteen U.S. cities. **Sample answers are given.**

U.S. City	Latitude	January Mean Temperature
Albany, New York	42:40 N	20.7°F
Albuquerque, New Mexico	35:07 N	34.3°F
Anchorage, Alaska	61:11 N	14.9°F
Birmingham, Alabama	33:32 N	41.7°F
Charleston, South Carolina	32:47 N	47.1°F
Chicago, Illinois	41:50 N	21.0°F
Columbus, Ohio	39:59 N	26.3°F
Duluth, Minnesota	46:47 N	7.0°F
Fairbanks, Alaska	64:50 N	−10.1°F
Galveston, Texas	29:14 N	52.9°F
Honolulu, Hawaii	21:19 N	72.9°F
Las Vegas, Nevada	36:12 N	45.1°F
Miami, Florida	25:47 N	67.3°F
Richmond, Virginia	37:32 N	35.8°F
Tucson, Arizona	32:12 N	51.3°F

Sources: www.indo.com and www.nws.noaa.gov/climateohtml

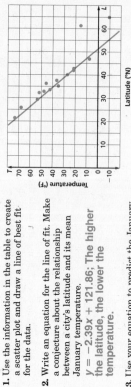

1. Use the information in the table to create a scatter plot and draw a line of best fit for the data.

2. Write an equation for the line of fit. Make a conjecture about the relationship between a city's latitude and its mean January temperature.
$y = -2.39x + 121.86$; **The higher the latitude, the lower the temperature.**

3. Use your equation to predict the January mean temperature of Juneau, Alaska, which has latitude 58:23 N. −17.7°F

4. What would you expect to be the latitude of a city with a January mean temperature of 15°F? 44:42 N

5. Was your conjecture about the relationship between latitude and temperature correct? **Yes; as the latitude increases, the temperature decreases.**

6. Research the latitudes and temperatures for cities in the southern hemisphere instead. Does your conjecture hold for these cities as well? **Yes.**

© Glencoe/McGraw-Hill

322

Glencoe Algebra 1

Lesson 5-7

Chapter 5 Assessment Answer Key

1. __B__

2. __C__

3. __A__

4. __D__

5. __D__

6. __B__

7. __C__

8. __D__

9. __A__

10. __C__

11. __C__

12. __C__

13. __B__

14. __B__

15. __B__

16. __A__

17. __B__

18. __A__

19. __D__

20. __D__

B: _____7_____

1. __A__

2. __A__

3. __B__

4. __B__

5. __D__

6. __A__

7. __C__

8. __B__

9. __D__

10. __C__

11. __D__

(continued on the next page)

Answers

Chapter 5 Assessment Answer Key

Form 2A *(continued)*
Page 326

12. __C__

13. __B__

14. __C__

15. __B__

16. __D__

17. __C__

18. __A__

19. __B__

20. __C__

B: __$\dfrac{17}{3}$__

Form 2B
Page 327

1. __D__

2. __C__

3. __A__

4. __B__

5. __B__

6. __B__

7. __D__

8. __B__

9. __B__

10. __A__

11. __C__

Page 328

12. __B__

13. __A__

14. __B__

15. __A__

16. __D__

17. __C__

18. __A__

19. __B__

20. __C__

B: __−21__

Chapter 5 Assessment Answer Key

Form 2C
Page 329

1. ___1___

2. ___0___

3. ___$-\dfrac{11}{9}$___

4. ___-25___

5. ___about -0.49___

6.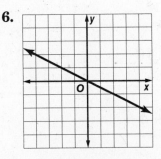

7. ___$d = 3t$; 36 mi___

8. ___$y = 0.10x + 28.75$___

9. ___$5x + 7y = 14$___

10. ___$y = \dfrac{2}{3}x - 2$___

11.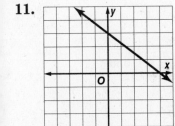

12. ___$y = \dfrac{3}{2}x - \dfrac{1}{2}$___

13. ___$x = -6$___

14. ___$y - 8 = \dfrac{1}{3}(x + 2)$___

15. ___$12x + 7y = -16$___

16. ___$y = 3x - 10$___

17. ___$y = -2x + 1$___

18. ___$y = \dfrac{2}{3}x - 4$___

19.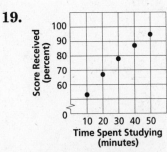

20. ___Sample answer: Using data points (20, 67) and (40, 87), $y = x + 47$; 82___

B: ___$\ell = 1.2t + 1.8$; 6 years___

Answers

Chapter 5 Assessment Answer Key

Form 2D
Page 331

1. _____ 0 _____

2. _____ $-\dfrac{3}{5}$ _____

3. _____ **undefined** _____

4. _____ 1 _____

5. _____ about $-\dfrac{1}{3}\%$ _____

6.
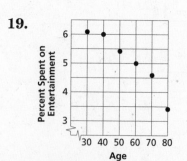

7. _____ $\dfrac{1}{2}h$ _____

8. $y = 2.50x + 4.95$

9. _____ $x - y = 2$ _____

10. _____ $y = -\dfrac{2}{3}x - 2$ _____

11.

Page 332

12. _____ $y = -5x + 29$ _____

13. _____ $x = 5$ _____

14. _____ $y = \dfrac{4}{3}(x - 3)$ _____

15. _____ $2x + 3y = -1$ _____

16. _____ $y = \dfrac{3}{4}x - \dfrac{5}{4}$ _____

17. _____ $y = -3x + 18$ _____

18. _____ $y = -\dfrac{1}{4}x + 4$ _____

19.

20. **Sample answer:**
Using data points (30, 6.1) and
(70, 4.7), $y = -0.035x + 7.15$;
about 4.9

B: _____ $y = \dfrac{6}{5}x - 6$ _____

Chapter 5 Assessment Answer Key

Form 3
Page 333

1. $-\dfrac{9}{13}$

2. undefined

3. -13

4. $\dfrac{70}{13}$

5. about 690 people/yr

6.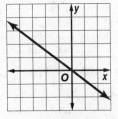

7. 60

8. $y - 1 = -\dfrac{3}{5}(x - 2)$

9. $2x + y = 1$

10.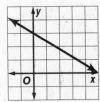

11. $2x + 3y = 6$

12. $y + 2 = -\dfrac{2}{3}x$

Page 334

13. $y = 3x - 8$

14. $y = \dfrac{5}{2}x - 11$

15. $y = -\dfrac{3}{5}x + \dfrac{26}{5}$

16. $y = 6$

17. $x = 3$

18. $y = -\dfrac{4}{3}x - 9$

19. $y = \dfrac{3}{5}x - 6$

20. $y = 5$

21.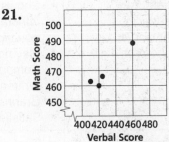

22. Positive; a verbal score is closely associated with the math score

23. Sample answer:
Using data points
(424, 466) and (460, 488)
$y = 0.6x + 211.6$; about 479

24. Sample answer:
$y = 52.99 + 0.12(x - 200)$

25. $y = -0.5x + 2$

B: 9

Answers

Chapter 5 Assessment Answer Key

Page 335, Open-Ended Assessment
Scoring Rubric

Score	General Description	Specific Criteria
4	**Superior** A correct solution that is supported by well-developed, accurate explanations	• Shows thorough understanding of the concepts of *slope, various forms of a linear equation, graphing lines from an equation, scatter plots, correlation,* and *predicting data.* • Uses appropriate strategies to solve problems. • Computations are correct. • Written explanations are exemplary. • Graphs are accurate and appropriate. • Goes beyond requirements of some or all problems.
3	**Satisfactory** A generally correct solution, but may contain minor flaws in reasoning or computation	• Shows an understanding of the concepts of *slope, various forms of a linear equation, graphing lines from an equation, scatter plots, correlation,* and *predicting data.* • Uses appropriate strategies to solve problems. • Computations are mostly correct. • Written explanations are effective. • Graphs are mostly accurate and appropriate. • Satisfies all requirements of problems.
2	**Nearly Satisfactory** A partially correct interpretation and/or solution to the problem	• Shows an understanding of most of the concepts of *slope, various forms of a linear equation, graphing lines from an equation, scatter plots, correlation,* and *predicting data.* • May not use appropriate strategies to solve problems. • Computations are mostly correct. • Written explanations are satisfactory. • Graphs are mostly accurate. • Satisfies the requirements of most of the problems.
1	**Nearly Unsatisfactory** A correct solution with no supporting evidence or explanation	• Final computation is correct. • No written explanations or work is shown to substantiate the final computation. • Graphs may be accurate but lack detail or explanation. • Satisfies minimal requirements of some of the problems.
0	**Unsatisfactory** An incorrect solution indicating no mathematical understanding of the concept or task, or no solution is given	• Shows little or no understanding of most of the concepts of *slope, various forms of a linear equation, graphing lines from an equation, scatter plots, correlation,* and *predicting data.* • Does not use appropriate strategies to solve problems. • Computations are incorrect. • Written explanations are unsatisfactory. • Graphs are inaccurate or inappropriate. • Does not satisfy the requirements of problems. • No answer may be given.

Chapter 5 Assessment Answer Key

Page 335, Open-Ended Assessment
Sample Answers

In addition to the scoring rubric found on page A28, the following sample answers may be used as guidance in evaluating open-ended assessment items.

1a. After drawing a graph, students should explain that they can use the two points on the graph to determine the slope. This can be done by counting squares for the rise and run of the line or by using the coordinates of the points in the slope formula.

1b. The slope is the value of m in the slope-intercept form $y = mx + b$. By substituting the value of m and the coordinates of one of the points for x and y, the value of b can be found and an equation written using m and b. The slope and either ordered pair can be used to write the point-slope form of an equation. The standard form of an equation is an algebraic manipulation of either of the other two forms of equations. See students' equations for the line drawn.

2a. In order to graph the line through $(-2, 3)$ you need to know the slope of the line, another point on the line, or the equation of the line.

2b. If you knew the slope of the line, you could plot another point using the rise and run on a coordinate plane. If you knew another point, you could graph that point and draw a line through $(-2, 3)$ and the other point. If you knew the equation of the line, you could use the slope-intercept form of the equation to find the slope and intercept for graphing or you could use the equation and substitution to find another point on the line.

3a. The points have a strong negative correlation. This means that as x increases, y decreases.

3b. One example is the longer a candle burns, the shorter it gets. Another is the longer you run a car, the less gasoline is left in the tank.

3c. See students' work.

4a.

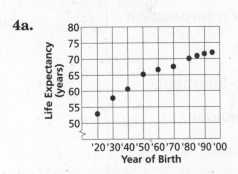

4b. While students' knowledge from other experiences may lead them to that conclusion, there may be other factors that contribute to increased longevity. The information on the graph only leads us to claim that life expectancy is increasing.

4c. A regression equation calculated by a graphing calculator would yield a prediction of 78.9 years. However, students may look at the era since 1980 and notice that each 5-year period is about 0.3 year less than the previous 5-year period increase. This pattern would yield a prediction of about 75.9 years.

Answers

Chapter 5 Assessment Answer Key

Vocabulary Test/Review
Page 336

1. perpendicular lines; parallel lines

2. constant of variation

3. scatter plot

4. family of graphs

5. rate of change

6. linear interpolation

7. slope

8. slope-intercept

9. point-slope

10. standard

11. Sample answer: A line of fit is a line that comes close to the data points for a scatter plot, even if all the data points do not lie on that line.

12. Sample answer: Linear extrapolation is the process of using a linear equation to predict a y value for an x value that lies beyond the extremes of the domain of the relation.

Quiz (Lessons 5–1 and 5–2)
Page 337

1. $\dfrac{2}{9}$

2. $\dfrac{7}{4}$

3. undefined

4. 5 students/yr

5. $285

Quiz (Lessons 5–3 and 5–4)
Page 337

1. $y = \dfrac{1}{4}x - 5$

2. $y = -\dfrac{4}{11}x + \dfrac{58}{11}$

3.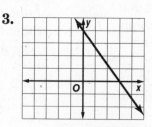

4. $h = 3y + 48$ for h in inches or $h = 0.25y + 4$ for h in feet

5. C

Quiz (Lessons 5–5 and 5–6)
Page 338

1. $y - 6 = -\dfrac{1}{3}(x - 3)$

2. $y = -x + 7$

3. $y + 1 = 0$

4. $y = -\dfrac{1}{3}x + \dfrac{14}{3}$

5. $y = -\dfrac{4}{9}x + 3$

Quiz (Lesson 5–7)
Page 338

1–2.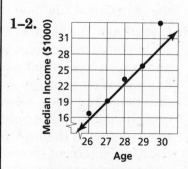

3. Positive; the older you get, the greater your income.

4. Sample answer: Using data points (27, 19.1) and (29, 25.8), $y = 3.35x - 71.35$

5. Sample answer: $35,850